The best
value health
book ever

THE BEST VALUE

Health

BOOK EVER

Kate Cook & Sally Brown

infinite ideas

Careful now

We want you to have a healthy and rewarding life but that doesn't mean we want to live it for you. You're a grown up now so it's up to you to take responsibility for your own health and wellbeing. Any alteration in the way you go about your life can affect its quality so you should consult your doctor or healthcare provider before changing your diet, undertaking any kind of change to your exercise routine or taking any nutritional supplements. If you have any health problems of any nature – physical, emotional or mental – always consult the appropriate healthcare providers.

Although the contents of this book were checked at the time of going to press, the World Wide Web is constantly changing. This means the publisher and author cannot guarantee the contents of any of the websites mentioned in the text.

Acknowledgements

Infinite Ideas would like to thank the following authors for their contributions to this book: Linda Bird, Sally Brown, Eve Cameron, Dr Ruth Chambers, Kate Cook, Peter Cross, Dr Sabina Dosani, Mandy Francis, Dr Rob Hicks, Clive Hopwood, Lynn Huggins-Cooper, Giles Kime, Steve Shipside, Karen Williamson and Elisabeth Wilson.

First published in 2007 by
The Infinite Ideas Company Limited
36 St Giles
Oxford
OX1 3LD
United Kingdom
www.infideas.com

Reprinted 2007

A CIP catalogue record for this book is available from the British Library

ISBN 978-1-904902-86-7

Brand and product names are trademarks or registered trademarks of their respective owners.

Text designed and typeset by Baseline Arts Ltd, Oxford
Cover design by Cylinder
Printed in India

Brilliant ideas

Brilliant features

Each chapter of this book is designed to provide you with an inspirational idea that you can read quickly and put into practice straight away.

Throughout you'll find three features that will help you to get right to the heart of the idea:

- *Here's an idea for you* Give it a go – right here, right now – and get an idea of how well you're doing so far.

- *Defining ideas* Words of wisdom from masters and mistresses of the art, plus some interesting hangers-on.

- *How did it go?* If at first you do succeed try to hide your amazement. If, on the other hand, you don't this is where you'll find a Q and A that highlights common problems and how to get over them.

Introduction

'Health' and 'healthy' mean different things to different people. Most of us would like to be healthier. For some of us that will mean conquering a persistent health problem such as diabetes, insomnia or high blood pressure while for others it means building up the strength and stamina to run the London Marathon. However far you want to go in the quest for better health we hope you will find some new, exciting and inspirational tips here.

If you do have a persistent problem then you may well have spent many years trailing round doctors' surgeries, taking various tests and you may even have visited a few complementary practitioners too. You have probably picked up snippets of information from magazines, newspaper articles and television programmes, but it's often hard to separate the great ideas from the fads.

We can't pretend that we're able to take the place of qualified professionals but what you will find in this book are tried and tested ideas from real people, that can make a genuine impact on your health and well-being. Several of our authors are doctors, so you can also be confident that the information here is good medical sense. This book is full of sensible diet tips, helpful exercise ideas and tried and tested solutions to common medical problems and in many cases our authors know what works because they've tried it themselves and achieved great results.

Don't feel you need to try all the tips in order. This book has been designed so that you can dip into it anywhere, any time. If you have a particular problem area – back pain, stress, PMS – then turn straight to the relevant idea to sort it out. Other ideas will give you more general advice for wellbeing and vitality. Most importantly we hope you enjoy reading the book. Good health can be yours – sleep well, eat well, keep an eye on your bad habits (you know what they are) and above all enjoy life.

1

Salt away

When is it good to be down and out? When it's salt you're talking about – cut it down or cut it out...

Too much salt can lead to high blood pressure — increasing your risk of heart disease. So the less salt you have, the better.

Reducing salt works. Having more salt in your diet triggers heart disease and raised blood pressure. We don't know why, but too much salt can give you acid reflux, too.

Most people consume around 10 g of salt a day – but if you like salty food, you could be eating twice as much. Try to have less than 6 g of salt in total per day: that's about one level teaspoon. You probably don't have much of a clue about how much salt is in the food you eat – how much is in your basic food, not just what you add to your cooking or sprinkle on afterwards, and it can be fiddly to find out. Processed foods – such as canned soups, sausages, meat pies, take-aways and other ready prepared meals – are stuffed with salt. Bread, and some cereals, have salt added to heighten their taste, and these are foods you might not suspect of being high in salt. The ones which are typically full of salt are crisps, nuts, pork pies and pizzas.

Salt is often given as sodium on food labels. This isn't very helpful, but 2.5 g of sodium is equivalent to 6 g of salt, and 0.5 g or more of sodium per 100 g of food is

Here's an idea for you...

Get hold of a salt calculator to help encourage you to cut your salt intake. The credit-card-sized calculator can help you to measure your salt consumption and convert sodium to salt quantities. If you can't find one in the shops, they're available online.

an awful lot of salt; less than 0.1 g of sodium per 100 g of food is a little salt. If you go and look at a tin of baked beans, you'll probably find it contains about 1 g of sodium per serving, and remember to take the size of helping into account and not just the concentration of salt. Foods like marmite have a high salt content, but you only use a little bit, whereas a helping of baked beans is two-fifths of the maximum salt intake you should have in an entire day.

Here's some advice on cutting down.

First, cut out or reduce the 25% or so of your daily salt intake that comes from adding salt to food while you're cooking or eating. If you can't, consider switching to a low-salt alternative: these contain up to two-thirds less sodium by substituting potassium chloride – unless there's a reason you should avoid extra potassium in your diet. You can cut down gradually; you're trying to reverse the bad habits of a lifetime, after all. Leave out foods that are high in salt and move to ones that are healthier. This might involve a complete rethink of your diet or a simple change to alternative cereals or breads, for example. Avoid salty snacks, choosing a piece of fruit or carrot instead (you angel, you!) and buy canned food that states 'no added salt'. Make your own sauces from scratch rather than buying prepared ones which are high in salt. Shake the salt cellar once instead of twice or more. As you get used to less salt you might actually find that your food is tastier: too much salt can mask the flavour.

Secondly, remember that what you see is what you get. Packaged food has nutritional information on the labels, so read them before you put your shopping in your trolley. Look at

'**Good habits result from resisting temptation.'**
Ancient proverb

Defining idea...

the amount per serving for pre-prepared food, and not just at the amount per 100 g which will probably be much less (and bear in mind that some manufacturers' ideas of what a 'serving' is may not be the same as yours). For crisps and nuts look at the amount per packet; assume you'll eat the lot...

There are lots of myths around salt. Don't believe things like these:

- 'Posh salt is better for you than table salt.' No, it isn't! It doesn't matter how much the salt costs or where it comes from. It's the sodium it contains that does the damage.
- 'You need to use more salt when it's hot or when you get overheated from playing sports because you sweat it out.' Not true. You lose a small amount of salt in sweat and that's easily covered by your everyday food.

And there are lots more where those came from. Don't fall for them.

How did
it go?

Q I have sprinkled salt over my food for the last thirty years. How can I break my bad habit?

A   *Try adding mixed herbs, garlic or ginger while cooking to give your food more flavour. That way you won't need to sprinkle salt on at the table or even in cooking. Your taste buds will adapt to the change pretty quickly and soon you won't miss it. Put your salt at the back of a cupboard and only bring it out for guests. And don't put those little salt packets on your tray in canteens or cafés – once you're at the table it will be too much bother to go back to collect the salt and you'll do without. Promise!*

Q Is sea salt lower in sodium than common salt?

A   *No. Sea salt is sodium chloride too, but extracted from the sea rather than from the ground.*

Q What kind of low-salt ready meals can I eat that are easy to cook up when I'm home late?

A   *Anything, provided you don't buy them; make up your own and you'll know what's gone into them. Use lemon, limes and oranges to flavour meat dishes. Make a stash of salt-free stock from stewing vegetables and use it for making sauces and gravy for your main meals and casseroles. Freeze tubs of that too.*

2

Check it out!

Ever fantasised about making an appointment with your doctor and saying, 'Check everything out, please'?

Getting a health all-clear is a great way to motivate you to maintain a healthier lifestyle in the future.

Regular health checks are essential if you want to live a long and healthy life because you've got a much better chance of curing many serious diseases – including cancer – if you catch them early. Unfortunately, doctors have neither the time nor the resources to run random tests for every patient, which leaves you with two options. You could opt for one of the many screening packages on offer from private health companies (which can be costly). Alternatively, there are many self-checks you can easily do at home which can help you assess whether you do really need to see your doctor for further investigation.

The first check is to find out if you're overweight or obese. Obesity is linked with a host of diseases such as cancer, diabetes and heart disease. To check if you're in the healthy weight range, calculate your body mass index (you'll probably need a calculator). First, measure your height in metres. Multiply this figure by itself (e.g. 1.5 m × 1.5 m). This gives your height squared. Now measure your weight in kilograms. Divide your weight by your height squared. This gives you your body

Here's an idea for you...

If you don't know what your cholesterol level is, make an appointment with your doctor to get tested this week. Alternatively buy a cholesterol self-test from pharmacies which involves taking a small sample of blood from your finger tip and placing it on a test strip. Results are then compared to a colour chart in three minutes.

mass index. A healthy figure is 20–25. A BMI of 25–30 is overweight; 30–40 is obese BMI, and above 40 is very obese. (If you don't want to do the maths, there's a BMI calculator on www.cyberdiet.com.)

If you are overweight, it's worth considering a diabetes test. The average person lives with diabetes for sixteen years before diagnosis – by which time the disease may have caused heart and kidney damage. You're more at risk if you have a family member with the disease, you're over fifty or overweight. You can buy a self-test for diabetes cheaply at most pharmacies, but be sure to follow it up with a medical appointment if it's positive.

Next, listen to your heartbeat. Heart disease is a massive killer, but you don't need to book in for an ECG (electrocardiogram) to check out your heart – simply observe what it's like after physical exertion such as climbing stairs. See your doctor if your heartbeat is irregular, or takes a long time to come back to normal.

If you've no idea what your blood pressure is, now's the time to find out. Hypertension, or high blood pressure, is the biggest cause of stroke or heart disease so it could be worth buying a digital blood pressure meter from pharmacies.

Now, some stuff for women only. Women over fifty are routinely invited for a mammogram every three years. But more than 90% of breast cancers are found by women themselves. The key is to be aware of what's normal for your breasts – don't get obsessive about checking them, but feel for any lumps once a month or so when you're in the bath or shower. And make sure you report anything unusual, such as nipple discharge or puckering of the skin of the breast, to your doctor.

'Be careful about reading health books. You may die of a misprint.'
MARK TWAIN

Defining
idea...

Also for women: don't skip your smear test. A smear test checks for cell changes on the cervix which could, if left untreated, lead to cervical cancer. Women aged between 20 and 64 should have a smear test every three to five years, although you may be tested more regularly if you have shown any signs of abnormal cells in the past. Men, meanwhile, should see their GP for a prostate test if they suddenly start peeing more frequently.

Checking your health doesn't have to be just another chore – it can even be fun if you rope in a partner. How about an all-over massage, with some mole checking thrown in? Look out for moles which have changed shape or colour, seem bigger, bleed or are itchy. Some men are also more than happy to take over checking their partner's breasts and also prefer their partners to check their testicles for unusual lumps that may be testicular cancer. Any excuse, eh, boys?

How did it go?

Q   **I've been putting on weight lately and I swear I'm not eating any more than I used to. What test should I have?**

A   *A thyroid function test could help. An underactive thyroid gland can be the root of gradual weight gain, especially in women over fifty, and if left untreated can lead to heart problems. Other symptoms include tiredness, feeling cold and losing the hair. A blood test from your doctor can show if your thyroid is functioning properly. Once it's ruled out, your doctor can decide if you need further tests.*

Q   **Whatever disease I read about, I'm convinced I've got. My doctor is sick of the sight of me. What can I do?**

A   *In years gone by, you'd simply be labelled a hypochondriac. But these days, we've got a new name for what you're suffering – health anxiety. It's thought to be on the increase thanks to an overload of information about health now available on the internet, on TV, in newspapers, magazines and books. The trouble is that many diseases – take diabetes for example – have symptoms which can also be caused by simply leading a stressful life. So it's easy to jump to wrong conclusions, but if you're doing this more and more often and feel like it's affecting your life, then see your doctor (again!). Explain what's happening; your doctor may decide to refer you to a cognitive behavioural therapist to help you get your fears into perspective.*

3

Yoga

Yoga is about being rather than doing. It's non-competitive and a great balancer for the type of exercise you might do at the gym.

Not so long ago, if you admitted you did yoga you'd have been classed as a New Age weirdo and given a wide berth. Today, if you're not into yoga you're the weird one. So, get with the programme!

Although yoga has evolved to incorporate quite a few different types, you're missing the point if you're using yoga to 'get a work-out'. Check out www.yogapoint.com for a guide to all the different types of yoga and pick the one that sounds interesting for you. You might want to experiment with the different types by going to a few classes. Or ask around, as friends might be able to give you advice.

In essence though, all types of yoga are about using the body and breathing to help calm the mind in order to produce a feeling of wellbeing. Yoga is a great stress buster if ever there was one and it's easy to do at any age so it's never too late to start. Flexibility is a vital component, both physically and mentally – a flexible mind

Here's an idea for you...

As an alternative to hiring a private teacher, which can be quite expensive, club together with a couple of friends for some really worthwhile tuition in a small group once a week. You can always go to classes at the gym the rest of the time.

equals a flexible body. Yoga generally uses asanas (postures) that usually retain their ancient names: the fish, the bridge, the bow, the scorpion, etc. They are believed to bring benefits to different areas of the body and are held for a period of time to stretch and strengthen muscles. The shoulder-stand asana, for example, is said to massage the thyroid and bring benefits to the mind through improving blood circulation to the head. Worth a try? The simplest asana is the corpse position, which involves lying down on your back on the floor with your eyes closed. Your breathing should be slow and steady, and your arms should be held at a 45-degree angle away from the body.

...and another

If you're disciplined and motivated use tapes and DVDs at home. It obviously depends on the type of yoga you settle on, but Sivananda centres offer good tapes.

Yoga is really a lifestyle rather than simply an exercise discipline. It incorporates 'proper' breathing or relaxation and a 'proper' diet. It's powerful stuff that's deceptively simple and amazingly dynamic. A proper diet, according to the yogis, is usually a vegetarian diet comprising Sattic foods such as wholemeal grains and fresh fruit and vegetables. Diet as a whole is divided up into three main sections: Sattic foods, which I've already mentioned; Rajasic foods, which are hot and bitter foods (e.g. coffee, tea, chocolate, salt, strong herbs, fish) that are considered to destroy the mind–body equilibrium; and Tamasic foods (e.g. meat, alcohol, garlic, onions), which neither benefit the mind nor the body as they encourage a sense of inertia. Stale or unripe food is also considered Tamasic.

Defining idea...

'Asanas make one firm, free from maladies, light of limb.'
Hatha Yoga Prdipika

Defining idea...

'The soul that moves in the world of senses in harmony...finds rest in quietness.'
Bhagavad Gita

How did it go?

Q **I'd really like to take yoga further. What do you suggest?**

A *Why not go on a yoga holiday? There's a lot of them about, but I like The Hill That Breathes (www.thehillthatbreathes.com), which combines yoga with great food and wine in the beautiful Italian countryside. Otherwise, good books that I like include The Book of Yoga – The Complete Step-by-Step Guide by The Sivananda Centre, which has loads of pictures.*

Q **I'm pregnant. Can I still do yoga?**

A *Yes, but do ask a qualified yoga teacher which exercises are suitable and which ones you should avoid, as it's really important not to strain yourself. There are often special pregnancy classes and I'd suggest you check out Sivananda (www.sivananda.org), which has a centre in most countries and many major cities.*

4

The incredible bulk

**It comes from plants and cannot be digested, nor does it
provide any calories or energy. So what, you may well ask,
is the point of fibre? Actually it's fascinating. How long
have you got?**

Fibre is about a lot more than chewing on
bran flakes to keep you regular. As well as its
myriad health benefits, fibre can also help you
stay slim.

Generally people with high fibre diets weigh less than those who don't each much
fibre. This could be due to the fact that fibre-rich foods are filling. And if you're full
you don't feel the need to overeat or snack on treats. A recent paper on weight loss
in the US confirmed that low fat diets with plenty of complex carbohydrates, fruit
and vegetables are naturally high in fibre and low in calories and as such lead to
weight loss. One study even reported that following this kind of eating model, the
carbohydrates could be consumed freely and weight would still be lost.

Here's an idea for you...

Drink a litre of juice a day: it's around 400 calories. Drink a litre of water and eat a couple of oranges instead. It will save you calories and give you more fibre. Fruit juice is healthy and full of vitamins and counts as one of five a day fruit and vegetable portions. It's also high in sugars, albeit natural ones.

The benefits of fibre, or to give it its new, proper name, non-starch polysaccharides, have been known for thousands of years. Hippocrates (known as the father of medicine) advised his wealthy patients to follow the example of their servants and eat brown bread rather than white for example, for its salutary effect on the bowel. Now we know more about fibre itself.

There are two kinds of fibre, soluble and insoluble. They are not nutrients in themselves as they are not digested for the most part, but both have important jobs to do. Soluble fibre lowers blood cholesterol levels and also slows the absorption of glucose into the bloodstream ensuring there isn't a sudden rise in blood sugar levels. Although most plant foods combine soluble and insoluble fibre, the former is found particularly in oats and oat bran, barley, brown rice, beans and pulses, and fruit and vegetables. Insoluble fibre keeps things moving along in your digestive system. Look away now if bottom and bowel business makes you feel a little uncomfortable and fidgety. It acts a bit like a sponge and soaks up water to expand the bulk of your waste products (the faeces). Basically with dietary fibre your stools are softer and move along easily, which helps to avoid constipation and piles and also protects against rectal and colon cancers. The best sources of insoluble fibre are wheat, whole grain breads and cereals, corn, green beans and peas and the skins of fruits such as apples.

CAN YOU HAVE TOO MUCH OF A GOOD THING?

It's recommended that we eat around 18 g of fibre a day, which most of us barely manage. We don't manage it because we eat more refined carbohydrates (white, processed foods and sugars) and don't eat enough fruit and vegetables. But the benefits are clear to see. When you increase your fibre consumption, make sure you drink plenty of water. You might also find that you retain some fluid at first, making you look and feel a little heavier. And there may be a bit of wind! This is temporary though as you get used to the new foods in your diet. Increasing your activity levels helps as it stimulates the muscles in the torso, helping speedier elimination – you don't want all that waste hanging around. There's some evidence that very high intakes of wheat bran can interfere with the absorption of iron and calcium, but it would need to be consistently high to really cause problems (though it can be a big issue for children and pregnant women). As new research suggests that high fibre consumption from a variety of sources affords a 40% lesser risk of bowel cancer and that women who eat plenty of fruit and vegetables and wholegrain cereals have a lower incidence of breast cancer, it makes sense to increase your dietary fibre and start chewing for health. And of course to keep hunger pangs at bay!

'There are food scares in Belgium involving everything from poultry to chocolate. To the despair of many worldwide, however, another millennium ends without any bad news about Brussels sprouts.'
FRANK McNALLY

Defining idea...

'A fruit is a vegetable with looks and money.'
P. J. O'ROURKE

Defining idea...

17

How did it go?

Q **I've got irritable bowel syndrome and I don't know whether to eat more bran and fibre or whether that will make it worse. Which is it?**

A *A high-fibre diet has always been recommended for IBS, but it doesn't work for everyone. Just as the actual symptoms of IBS can vary, so can the effects of fibre – it can make both diarrhoea and constipation worse for example. Mostly it seems that the problem is with wheat fibre, found in wholemeal bread and often in biscuits and cereal too. The only way to find out if it is this that's making things worse is to cut it out for at least a month, then slowly reintroduce some wholewheat into your diet and see what happens. You'll find you probably won't have problems with refined wheat products, such as white bread and pasta.*

Q **Could I take a fibre supplement?**

A *I wouldn't. Besides there are so many other nutrients in high fibre foods that you'd be missing out on – phytochemicals, minerals and antioxidants that all pack big health benefits.*

Q **Is there any way to avoid the windiness you get after eating pulses?**

A *If you're preparing them yourself, just make sure that they are thoroughly cooked (and, except for lentils and split peas, soaked overnight before cooking). I buy my pulses in cans because I can't be bothered with the lengthy preparation process. Just check they're canned in water only and don't have added sugar or salt. You could also try adding certain herbs to the pulse dishes you're making. Herbs that are claimed to help with wind include thyme, fennel, caraway, rosemary and lemon balm.*

5

End 'stop and collapse' syndrome

You take holidays. You know how important this is if you want to be stress-free.

And then you spend the first week in bed recovering from some dreaded lurgy. You've got leisure sickness — aka 'stop and collapse' syndrome.

The guy who first identified leisure sickness was a sufferer. Professor Ad Vingerhoets of Tilburg University noticed he always got ill on the first days of his holiday. So he did a study of nearly 2000 men and women aged between 16 and 87. And guess what? He wasn't alone. A small but significant number of his subjects regularly got ill at the weekend or on holidays. (I think his numbers must be an underestimate because most of the people I know are affected.) He discovered that those who got leisure sickness complained mainly of headaches, migraine, fatigue, muscular pains, nausea, colds and flu (especially common when going on holiday).

Those who got it shared certain characteristics: a high workload, perfectionism, eagerness to achieve, an over-developed sense of responsibility to their work – all of which make it difficult to switch off.

Here's an idea for you...

If you're prone to weekend sickness, try exercising on a Friday evening. Exercise is a stressor but one your body loves. This acts as a transition between work and time off, and helps you unwind quicker.

One theory is that those who work hard simply get so bored on holiday that they start to notice the symptoms they've been suppressing while at work. It could also be a case of 'mind over matter': we don't allow ourselves to get sick until the work is done. Yet another theory is that when you're working (stressed) your immune system is actually working better than it does when you're relaxing. When you relax, the immune system slows down, your defences relax, and kaboom!, you're calling the concierge for a doctor.

So what can you do about it? I'm going to suggest a two-pronged attack.

1. Support your local immune system

As a very bare minimum, eat a minimum of five fruit and veg a day and take a good-quality multivitamin and mineral supplement (I like Bioforce, Solgar, Viridian, Vitabiotics). If you drink too much alcohol or are a smoker, you also need more vitamin C – so supplement that too. I'm also a fan of echinacea, so give this a try as well (but read the instructions carefully: if you take it for too long, it loses its effectiveness).

2. Plan for holidays with military precision

You really need gradually to begin to wind down in the two weeks before you go.

Cue hollow laughter. You think I don't understand, but I do. In August 1998, the day before my holiday, I worked in the office from 6 a.m. until 11 p.m., went home, packed, slept for three hours, went back to the office at 4 a.m., worked until 8.30

and took a cab straight to the airport to get on a plane. That's not smart. That's borderline lunacy. So let's have no more of the workaholic nuttiness.

'Those who don't take the time to be well eventually have to find the time to be ill.'
ANON.

Defining idea...

Here are some ideas. (I am assuming everyone in your household has a valid passport. Young children's passports don't run as long as adults. Not sure about this? Go and check right now. This one small action could save you bucket loads of stress down the line.)

Three weeks before you go. Make a packing list. Write down everything you need to take with you and then allocate each lunchtime this week to completing any errands.

Two weeks before you go. Sort out work. Take a look at all your projects and decide at what stage you want to pass them over. Set goals with each project and allocate deadlines for reaching them, preferably all to be tied up the day before your last day.

One week before you go. Start packing. Put out your bags or suitcases in a spare room if you've got one and start the washing and ironing nightmare in the weekend before you go. Do a little packing each night. Also start winding up projects and writing up your handover notes to whichever colleague is taking over your responsibilities. You can always amend them on the last day if you get further with a project than you planned to. Amending is a lot better than starting them at 8.30 p.m. on your last day.

How did it go?

Q **I'm ill all year round. What should I do?**

A *People who successfully overcome leisure sickness often do this by making a major change of attitude, or change of lifestyle. The operative word here is 'change'. I'm going to say it again: you have to change. The symptoms of stress can be ignored or suppressed but eventually if you don't pay attention to what your body's telling you, you're going to get very sick indeed.*

Q **I simply can't switch off and that's why I get ill. When I'm away I'm constantly in touch with the office. How can I let go?**

A *Well, I heard of a woman who always holidayed several time zones away from her office to discourage phone calls 'They can never be bothered to work out the five hours forward or back thing,' she says. But that's no use if you phone the office. I could write reams about this, but it's quite simple really. Switching off means just that – phones, emails, texts, laptops. If you're a boss who can't trust your staff to get on – that's bad. Cognitive behavioural therapy could help. If you're an employee whose boss is so controlling he's calling you on holiday – that's worse. Talk to him. Or look for a new job.*

6

Act in time

If someone collapses and their heart stops, it could be up to you to do basic life support. Every second counts.

Be ready to help when someone collapses. It's as easy as ABC: that means check their Airway, Breathing and Circulation.

SO KNOW YOUR ABC

Phone the emergency services or get someone to a hospital right away if they have chest pain or discomfort, are short of breath, are in a cold sweat and seem to be having a heart attack. Suspect pain radiating from the chest to both arms, to the neck, jaw or stomach. If they've collapsed, buy time until help arrives by having a go at resuscitating them. You can't let someone lie there with no circulation, or they'll have irreversible brain damage.

Look about you. First, consider if you're safe where you are. Is there live electricity nearby or in contact with the casualty? Don't risk your safety in the middle of a busy road or on a precarious ledge; pull the person to a safer position before you start. OK, you know not to move someone if it's possible that they're unconscious, but weigh up the dangers. If it's no contest, then stay safe: pull them out of danger.

Here's an idea for you...

If you or a relative have had a heart attack in the past, consider buying a home defibrillator as a standby, and make sure there's someone around who could operate it. The home defibrillator can be used by virtually any ordinary person with less than an hour's training. One example of this kind (check out www.brompton.net) provides clear voice instructions that guide the user through every step of the defibrillation process. The defibrillator is a similar size and weight to a hardback book and does its own self-tests each day to ensure it's maintained and ready. The battery lasts for up to four years.

Try to get a response. Shout a command in an authoritative way. Squeeze their shoulders. Look into their mouth and check there are no foreign bodies. Place two fingers under the chin and put your other hand on their forehead, to push it back and extend and straighten the airway. Check if you can feel or hear their breathing for ten seconds, or if you can see their chest move as they breathe.

Still no luck? Then you'll have to start ventilating them. Seal your mouth over theirs while you continue to tip their head backwards and elevate their chin. Then blow into their mouth for two seconds, rest for four seconds and do it again. Check that their chest is rising and falling as you blow into their lungs.

Still no joy? They're not breathing by themselves? There's no sign of life? Check for a pulse in their neck or elsewhere – their wrist or heart. If there isn't one, you'll have to start doing chest compressions. Place the heel of your hand over the lower part of their breastbone, the width of two fingers above where the ribs join together. Keep your arms straight and use the weight of your body to press down. Aim to compress the chest by 4–5 cm, making fifteen compressions in quick sequence within about ten seconds. Continue to switch between giving two breaths and fifteen compressions until professional help arrives, or you see signs of life, or you're just too exhausted to carry on.

'In the midst of life we are in death.'
The Book of Common Prayer

Defining idea...

WHAT A DEFIBRILLATOR CAN DO

If the person's heart has stopped, it can be restarted with an electric shock given by a defibrillator. Two-thirds of people who have a cardiac arrest have an over-fast heart rhythm – ventricular fibrillation, or tachycardia – which can revert to normal with an electric charge from a defibrillation machine, if this is given quickly enough. These days you may be able or expected to use a defibrillator even if you're not a doctor or nurse. Automatic defibrillators are increasingly sited in public places such as supermarkets, shopping centres, train stations and aircraft.

A defibrillator discharges a fixed, high-voltage, direct current through pads attached to the person's chest. If there's a defibrillator standing by and it's down to you to use it, connect the leads to the pads before placing the pads on the bare chest, and don't put the pads over jewellery or you might cause a burn. When you press the button, no one should be in physical contact with the person or anything attached to them. If there's no response, try again, giving a maximum of three shocks.

How did
it go?

Q If someone's collapsed, do I just look into their mouth before starting or should I have a feel inside?

A . *Yes, you should, but have a good look too. When feeling, be careful: don't sweep your finger around as you might dislodge something and push it down further. And leave well-fitting dentures in place.*

Q I don't really like putting my lips to the mouth of someone I don't know; it seems a bit intimate. What's the alternative?

A *You could always get a key ring that carries a compact ventilation mask or keep a pocket-sized mask in the first aid kit in your car, office or home. Failing that, you could put a cotton or even paper handkerchief between your mouth and theirs. This will reduce the chances of you getting their saliva or vomit in your mouth while you're trying to resuscitate them. No one's been known to have caught HIV or the hepatitis B virus during mouth-to-mouth ventilation, mind.*

Q Any special precautions I should take when releasing the defibrillator charge, apart from not touching the person I'm using it on?

A *If you are in a wet environment make sure there's no water linking the person who has collapsed to your feet, or the electric charge you use to shock the person may be conveyed to you too.*

26

7

Moveable feasts

If you've run out of lunch box ideas – or simply don't know where to start – this chapter will give you the inspiration you're looking for.

A well-balanced packed lunch will provide your child with all the energy and nutrients she needs for a busy day at school or nursery.

Have you been making nothing but processed cheese sandwiches for the last few weeks? Do you always end up packing your little angel off to school with crisps and chocolate bars because you're worried she won't eat anything else? You are not alone.

According to a recent survey of children's lunch boxes, carried out by the Food Standards Agency, the contents of most packed lunches are way too high in saturated fats, sugar and/or salt. The same survey also showed that almost half of the lunch boxes examined did not contain fruit and that most of the lunches included heavily processed snacks, crisps, chocolate, biscuits and sugary fizzy drinks.

Whilst it's tempting to include junk food 'treats' in your child's lunch box – or hip, processed foods that have been heavily advertised on TV – don't. A meal that's poor in nutrients and high in salt, sugar and fat will sap your child's energy levels and mental alertness – and over time could even set the foundations for future health problems and obesity.

Here's an idea for you...

If you want to add a healthier sweet treat to your child's lunch, try making these banana and date muffins. Preheat the oven to 220C/400F/Gas 6. Line a twelve hole muffin tin with paper cases. Beat together 225 g/8 oz self raising flour, 1 tsp baking powder, 110 g/4 oz light muscovado sugar, 50 g/ 2 oz stoned, chopped dates, three mashed bananas, a large egg, 150 ml/1/4 pint skimmed milk and 4 tbsps sunflower oil. Pour into muffin cases and bake for 20–25 minutes until cooked through. Cool on a wire rack.

So if you're now at a loss as to what to give your child, don't worry – it really is quite simple to put together a healthy packed lunch. Here's how:

A healthy lunch box should contain the following four basic elements. Try to vary the contents from day to day to ensure she gets a broad spectrum of nutrients.

1   A *portion of protein* (e.g. meat, fish, egg, cheese, beans, lentils, soya products, nuts, seeds and Quorn). Fill sandwiches, wraps, pitta bread or rolls with good quality roast chicken, turkey, ham, tuna, salmon, nut butter, cheese or egg – or add meat, fish or tofu to a pasta or rice salad.

2   *Some complex carbohydrates.* Complex carbohydrates are foods that offer a slower release of energy than refined carbs like white bread, white pasta, biscuits and cakes. Make sandwiches with wholegrain, multigrain or pitta bread and choose wholemeal pasta and brown rice for salads if possible.

3   *A calcium-rich food.* Cheese, yogurt, yogurt drinks, fromage frais and milk are all good sources of calcium – the mineral essential for healthy bones and teeth. Stick to whole milk dairy products for children under five. If your child can't tolerate dairy foods, consider alternative sources of calcium such as calcium enriched orange juice and soya milk.

4   *At least one portion of fruit and/or vegetables* for fibre, vitamins and minerals. Fiddly-to-eat items will tend to get left, so fill a small pot or freezer bag with peeled clementine segments or fresh pineapple pieces, grapes, sliced strawberries, carrot and cucumber batons, dried apricots or raisins

'Ask not what you can do for your country, ask what's for lunch.'
ORSON WELLES, actor, director

Defining idea...

Avoid

■ Ready-made cereal bars, muffins and flapjacks. They may sound healthy, but they're often high in sugar and fat and come in big portion sizes. Make your own smaller, healthier flapjacks or muffins instead, or choose fruit bread, fruit scones or malt loaf.

■ Savoury snack foods. Over-processed cheese and ham snacks and crisps are usually high in saturated fat and salt. Some savoury snack foods can contain a child's entire salt allowance in just one portion.

■ Fruit juice 'drinks' and fizzy pop. Anything that's labelled as a juice 'drink' is often little more than a fruit flavoured sugary drink – which, like fizzy pop may also contain artificial colourings and preservatives. Fruit juice that's made with 100% fruit, diluted 50:50 with water, is a better option – otherwise plain water, low sugar flavoured water, milk or a fruit smoothie.

A healthy lunch box may sound boring – but it doesn't have to be. Cut sandwiches into stars or animal shapes, then wrap in brightly coloured sandwich bags, sealed with stickers. Buy brightly coloured pots to store small quantities of fruit or snacks – and think variety. If your child has a different fruit/sandwich filling/yogurt or drink most days, she won't crave over-processed, salty, sugary, ready-made snacks.

It's also important to keep food cool until it's ready to be eaten, so an insulated lunch bag is a good idea. If you're organised, make the lunch the night before and store it in the fridge so everything is thoroughly chilled by morning. Alternatively freeze a carton of juice and add it to the lunch bag just before your child leaves the house. It will keep sandwiches cool and be defrosted and ready to drink by lunchtime.

How did it go?

Q   I feel like a real killjoy taking the crisps out of my son's lunch bag – especially when all his friends take crisps to school. Any suggestions?

A   *Well, let's be realistic – most foods are OK in moderation. If you really want to give him some crisps I suggest you just don't give him the whole bag. Decant a small portion into an airtight tub instead.*

Q   It's the salt content I worry most about – are some crisps a better bet than others?

A   *Yes, I suggest you buy 'salt and shake' crisps, the type that come with a separate bag of salt – and discard the salt.*

8

Game for a laugh

Laugh up to fifteen times a day and live up to eight years longer. True!

Laughter reduces stress, lowers blood pressure, relieves pain, oxygenates the blood and strengthens the immune system. So go on, have a chuckle.

Two hunters are out in the woods when one of them collapses. He doesn't seem to be breathing and his eyes are glazed. The other guy whips out his phone and calls the emergency services. He gasps, 'My friend is dead! What can I do?' The operator says, 'Calm down, I can help. First, let's make sure he's dead.' There is a silence, then a shot is heard. Back on the phone, the guy says, 'OK, operator, now what?'

That is officially the world's funniest joke – and if you laughed when you read it, you've given your immune system a huge boost. It seems laughter really is the best medicine and there's a raft of scientific studies to prove it.

If you've ever been stuck in a lift when someone's made a funny remark, you'll know that nothing relieves tension like laughing. Both physically and psychologically, laughter acts as a safety valve for the discharge of nervous tension.

Here's an idea for you...

Smile more and you'll feel happier. Studies on brain activity have shown that if you move your face into a smile, happy-chemicals are automatically released from your brain. So smiling more has the end result of, well, making you feel like smiling more. And it takes half as many muscles to smile as it does to frown.

Researchers have shown that laughter reduces the levels of the stress hormones cortisone and adrenaline and boosts the number of infection-fighting white T-cells in the body. During laughter, the heartbeat quickens and blood pressure rises; after laughter, both heart rate and blood pressure drop to a point that is lower than its initial resting rate. It's also thought that laughter may have evolved as a way of helping us to connect with fellow human beings and dissipating conflict. As comedian Alan Alda put it, 'When people are laughing, they're generally not killing one another.'

Doctors are now realising just how important laughter is to our health and are beginning to take jokes, er, seriously. In the 1960s, the award-winning writer Norman Cousins put his full recovery from a usually irreversible and crippling connective tissue disease down to a regimen that – among other therapies – included laughing at Marx Brothers movies every day. The book about his experience was an international bestseller.

Laughter may even improve your physical fitness. Have a real belly laugh and around 400 muscles of your body will move – it's like internal aerobics. It releases the same endorphins or pleasure chemicals in the brain as exercise, which induce feelings of well-being and relaxation. If you could keep up a belly laugh for a full hour, you could even laugh off as many as 500 calories.

The problem is that the older we get, the more it takes to make us laugh. At four we laugh 400 times a day. By age thirty, it's down to around fifteen. A small child doesn't need searing political satire to raise a smile. They'll laugh at any noise that vaguely resembles passing wind. Or just get three of them together, wait until one of them says 'wee-wee', then watch them all lie on their backs and laugh hysterically for ten minutes. When did we lose this sense of fun?

'Laughter is a tranquilliser with no side-effects.'
ARNOLD H. GLASGOW, psychologist

Defining idea...

Deciding to laugh more every day sounds like a simple way to live longer, but it's easier said than done. You can't force laughter. But you can polish up a rusty sense of humour by using it more often. If you've got in the habit of watching 24-hour news channels, get some DVDs of comedy films or a collection of *Simpsons* videos. Swap jokes by email. Hang out with some small kids.

To get you started, here's a joke.
Sherlock Holmes and Dr Watson are going camping. They pitch their tent under the stars and go to sleep. Sometime in the middle of the night Holmes wakes Watson up. 'Watson, look up at the stars, and tell me what you deduce.' Watson says, 'I see millions of stars and even if a few of those have planets, it's quite likely there are some planets like Earth, and if there are a few planets like Earth out there, there might also be life.' Holmes replies 'Watson, you idiot, someone stole our tent!'

'One laugh is worth two tablets.'
FREDDIE FRANKL, psychiatrist

Defining idea...

33

How did it go?

Q **I tried saying 'wee-wee' at work yesterday but no one laughed. Why is this?**

A *As every comedian will tell you, it's all in the timing. There's even a joke about it. A man goes to a prison and everyone is having lunch. Someone shouts out 'Twenty-three', and everyone falls about laughing. The man asks what's going on. Someone tells him. 'Because we've heard all the jokes we've numbered them all. Here, listen. Forty-eight!' It gets a big laugh. 'Let me try,' says the man. 'What's a good one?' 'Sixteen,' replies the inmate. The man shouts 'Sixteen!' There's no response. The other inmate leans over. 'It's not just the joke,' he says, 'it's the way you tell them.'*

Q **Sometimes if I really laugh I start to cry. Is this normal?**

A *Normal and pretty common – if the saying 'crying with laughter' is any indication. It's thought to be all tied up with stress release – having a good cry can be as big a tension reliever as a belly laugh. It just tends not to go down so well at the office.*

9

Breathe in, breathe out!

Proper breathing can be a forgotten art for people in stressful jobs, lives or relationships. And these days we often hold onto our breath out of sheer terror.

It's not called the life breath for nothing. With each breath we exchange carbon dioxide from inside the body with life-giving oxygen from outside. If this incredible process was interrupted for more than a few minutes, it would be curtains.

The partner to breathing is an amazingly reliable muscle: your heart. Oxygen-rich blood is pumped by the heart from the lungs via the arteries and small capillaries to all the cells of the body. This allows the cells to function. Carbon dioxide is then transported back to the heart through the veins and from there it's pumped to the lungs and we breathe it out. The whole process starts again with our next in-breath. Breathing is an amazing, miraculous process and it's worked so well that it hasn't changed one iota since we were running away from sabre-toothed beasties. Sometimes, however, that's just the problem.

Here's an idea for you...

When you're at the office, why not make your company's toilet your personal breathing booth?

We may think that we're civilised humans who know the difference between Armani and Woolworths, but the fact is that as far as our ancient intuitive response mechanisms go, we're just another animal fighting for our tiny space in the (concrete) jungle. We humans go through the same physiological reaction as a cat does when it's dumped in a barrel of freezing water or being chased by a dog, or as a mouse does when a cat is stalking it for that matter. When faced with what we perceive as a danger (this could be your tax bill, your boss or being late for work), we go into a state of hyperarousal known as the flight-or-fight system. You might think that hyperarousal sounds a bit saucy, but it actually means feelings like anxiety, rage or sheer blind terror. The resulting flight-or-fight mechanism is unbelievably clever and causes a rapid cascade of nervous-system firings and the release of powerful hormones like adrenaline. We become hyperaware of all our surroundings, the pupils of our eyes dilate to let in more light, the hair on our body stands up so that we become more sensitive to vibrations, the digestive system shuts down and the heart rate shoots up so that there's more blood available for legging it up a tree at top speed. And that's just for starters! Here's the technical part – you've just activated the sympathetic part of your autonomic nervous system. Impress your friends with that one!

This brings us back to breathing. Breathing centres you. It's almost impossible to be stressed if breathing is measured, calm and deep. Breathing overrides the powerful stress response and slows down the reaction of the autonomic nervous system. So, the good news is that you have some degree of control over how you react to stress.

BREATHING EXERCISES

'**Get wisdom and rest in peace.**'
SIVANANDA, the historical Buddha

Breathing exercises are deceptively simple and dynamically powerful. All you need is a few minutes a day to provide you with a powerful way of dealing with stress. There are hundreds of different exercises you could do. I'm going to give you just two for starters. Do them! Don't just read this and think it's for someone else. It's for you. It's for us all!

Exercise 1: observing the breath

Sit on a comfortable chair, making sure that your feet are on the ground. Close your eyes, rest one hand in your lap and place the other on your tummy. You should feel the tummy expanding as you breathe in and contracting as you breathe out. Breathe in deeply through your nose and silently count 'one'. Breathe out. Breathe in again and count 'two'. Do this for up to ten breaths and then do it the other way round. Breathe in. Breathe *out* and count 'one'. Breathe in. Breathe out and count 'two'. Do this for five rounds to start with, building up to ten. Do this once a day.

Exercise 2: anti-stress breath

Try this if you find yourself stressed out and in need of some immediate relief. Breathe in for four counts, hold for four counts and exhale for four counts. Remember to let the out-breath out slowly, not in a rush. Do this for about five cycles, being careful that you don't overdo it otherwise you could end up feeling a bit dizzy.

How did
it go?

Q   **I keep meaning to do the exercises because I know they'll be great and I'll really feel the difference, but I keep forgetting to do them.**

A   *Put the breathing exercises in your diary initially and write reminders on sticky notes on your bathroom mirror. It takes around twenty-one days to form a habit, but once you're into it, the habit will stick.*

Q   **How else can I make breathing a habit?**

A   *Try tapes – I find that meditation tapes are great for breathing exercises. There can be long silences, so don't let the guiding voice on the tape make you jump out of your skin when they start talking again! Try Andrew Weil's tape,* Breathing – The Masterkey to Self Healing.

10

Challenge cholesterol

There's been lots of talk, maybe too much talk, about cholesterol and how bad it is. But the time has come to separate the fats. Why, because not all fats are bad.

OK, let's have a quick science lesson. Fats provide energy, vitamins A, D and E, and also the essential fatty acids that the body cannot make for itself.

Cholesterol is required for cell membrane manufacture, the production of certain hormones and to assist in the digestive process. Around 25–33% of the cholesterol found within our bodies comes from the food that we eat. The remainder is made in the body when fats, particularly saturated fats, are converted by the liver into cholesterol.

Sounds good so far. Now here's the stinger. Any surplus bad cholesterol (called LDL-cholesterol) within the circulation may become oxidised, bombarded by free radicals that is, and dumped on the walls of the arteries. Imagine debris collecting in a water pipe. Slowly but surely the pipe gets clogged up, hindering the efficient flow of water. This is what happens when the arteries become furred up. Blood flow is restricted, and if it becomes completely obstructed the result is a heart attack or a stroke.

Here's an idea for you...

Over the next week total up how much fat you eat. You could also get your cholesterol level checked.

But here comes something to the rescue. There's also good cholesterol (called HDL-cholesterol) that removes cholesterol from the circulation.

The concern with high blood pressure is the damage it can cause to the arteries, which in turn contributes to heart attacks and strokes. Likewise high levels of bad cholesterol, and low levels of good cholesterol, increase the risk of blood vessel damage and subsequent heart disease. So, these risk factors have a common goal. Moreover, they work as a team, or a better term would be a terrorist cell, since it's damage and death they are working towards. High levels of bad cholesterol enhance the harmful effects of the other heart disease risk factors or cell members, namely obesity, smoking, poor activity levels, high blood pressure and stress, for example.

So how can you reduce your cholesterol level? What's important is to reduce the total amount of fat you eat, and to change the balance of the fats you eat so that you eat less saturated fat. Most people still eat too much fat in general, more than the recommended maximum 95 g a day for men, and maximum 70 g a day for women. Moreover, most of the fat eaten is saturated, and it's this that increases cholesterol levels the most. On the other hand, polyunsaturated fats can lower levels of bad cholesterol but may also lower levels of good cholesterol. Monounsaturated fats, however, can lower bad cholesterol while maintaining levels of good cholesterol.

Put simply, reducing the amount of fat, in particular the amount of saturated fat, eaten during the day means eating less fried foods, biscuits, cakes, cookies, pies and chips, and choosing reduced-fat products when possible – low-fat cream cheese, fat-free yoghurt, skimmed milk, low-fat crackers, for example.

'To be or not to be isn't the question. The question is how to prolong being.'
TOM ROBBINS

Defining idea...

Don't frown, here's some good news. You can eat more of the following – breakfast cereals with high soluble fibre content, porridge, legumes (e.g. beans, peas, lentils) and pectin-containing fruits (citrus fruit, apples and grapes) – these all help to lower cholesterol. Try cooking with olive oil too.

The current target figure for cholesterol is to have a level that is less than 5 mmol/l. The target level for bad cholesterol is less than 3 mmol/l. In the future these target levels may be reduced even further. You can get your cholesterol tested by your doctor and sometimes by your local pharmacist. This can help you to see how well you are doing, and knowing your level can act as a good motivator to eat healthily.

It's not just down to eating the right foods though. Regular exercise, and maintaining an ideal weight and losing some if you have to, can help to lower cholesterol levels too.

'We cannot become what we need to be by remaining what we are.'
MAX DEPREE

Defining idea...

How did
it go?

Q   Which foods have saturated fats?

A   *Generally speaking saturated fats are found in foods of animal origin, particularly meat and dairy products. Saturated fat also comes from plant sources too, for example palm oil and coconut oil. Some foods that contain beneficial monounsaturated fats are olive oil, rapeseed oil, avocado and nuts.*

Q   It's complicated, all these different types of fats. Can you simplify the issues?

A   *It's easy to tie yourself up in knots. If it's creating problems, rather than being helpful, during your next food shopping trip just try making the number of good-for-cholesterol foods – fruit, vegetables and high-fibre foods – greater than the number of higher-fat foods in your basket.*

Q   What about garlic?

A   *Some research shows that garlic helps lower cholesterol. It tastes great, so why not give it a try? Use as much fresh garlic as you can in cooking and in salad dressings. Some folks even chew raw garlic cloves. Eating a diet high in soluble fibre may also help to reduce the amount of cholesterol that is absorbed from your intestine into the bloodstream.*

Q   What about these foods that claim to help lower cholesterol?

A   *Some new designer or functional foods – margarines and yoghurts, for example – have over the past few years appeared on the shelves of food stores and claim to help lower cholesterol levels. They can help but are not a substitute for a low-fat diet, exercise and maintaining your optimum weight.*

11

Sick of food?

Everyone thinks they have a food allergy these days, but what's the truth behind this internal explosion? Here are the facts and fads of food allergy.

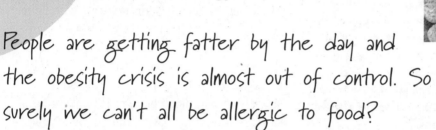

People are getting fatter by the day and the obesity crisis is almost out of control. So surely we can't all be allergic to food?

No, of course not, although listening to people around you you'd believe that everyone is. Many like to believe that it's an allergy that's responsible for problems in their life – constant tiredness, weight gain, poor sex life, even not being promoted. Some people think it's fashionable to have an allergy, thanks to celebrities and the media. And if you think that having an allergy is fashionable, then having a food allergy moves you smoothly into the VIP lounge and onto the A-list among this crowd.

The reality is that, although food allergy is becoming more common, it's nowhere near as common as people think. However, for those with true food allergy the problem is real, very real.

At the mildest end of the spectrum tingling or itching in or around the lips and mouth may be all that happens when the food culprit makes contact. For babies

Here's an idea for you...

Make a list of foods that are safe for you to eat. To make this easier, larger supermarkets often have 'free-from' lists available, as do major food manufacturers. Keep it with you, distribute it to friends and family – even pin it up on the noticeboard at work. By doing this you'll make shopping, cooking and eating much less hassle and you'll be reducing your risk of suffering allergic reactions.

with food allergy their gut is the likely victim, causing vomiting and diarrhoea. Now there's a good reason to keep 'the naughty foods away from oo then'. Symptoms of asthma and eczema may also be triggered by certain foods. At the other end of the spectrum severe allergic, or anaphylactic, reaction, with light-headedness, difficulty breathing, a sense of impending doom, shock and loss of consciousness, puts survival in the hands of immediate emergency treatment. So if you were ever thinking of using food allergy as a reason to escape paying the restaurant bill, think again.

The parts of food responsible for causing allergic reactions, the allergens, are usually proteins. Even after cooking or digestion many of these allergens can still cause reactions. The most common offenders are the proteins in cow's milk, eggs, peanuts, wheat, soy, fish, shellfish and tree nuts. These are responsible for up to 90% of all allergic reactions. In children, the following six foods cause the majority of food allergy reactions: milk, eggs, peanuts, wheat, soy and tree nuts. In adults, four foods cause the majority of allergic reactions: peanuts, tree nuts, fish and shellfish.

OK, let's take a look at the basics. If you have already been diagnosed with a true food allergy you should know this like the back of your hand, and if you don't then shame on you! If you don't have a food allergy, and I'm talking

'Give me neither poverty nor riches; feed me with food convenient for me.'
Proverbs 30:8

Defining idea...

about a true food allergy, then this is important for you too, because someone around you will have a true food allergy and you need to know what to do if things go pear-shaped.

So step one: avoid the food. Doh! Pretty obvious, even to the Homer Simpsons among you. True, but it's not so easy as it sounds. Why? Because the protein responsible may be an ingredient. So step two is to ask about ingredients so that you don't get caught out by hidden food allergens. This is especially important when you are eating away from home since getting caught out when you're playing away can leave you red faced. And if you're the host, don't forget to ask your guests if they have any allergies. Step three: read food labels carefully and get familiar with what the terms used mean. For example, egg white is often listed as albumin, and casein is always made from milk. Hopefully before too long that well-known food manufacturer cop-out, 'may contain traces of ...' will be replaced by something more helpful so that those with food allergy have a greater choice of foods. And so to step four: be prepared for action if an allergic reaction erupts.

How did it go?

Q   **What should I do when my friend, Al Lergic, comes to stay? I don't know what foods to avoid.**

A   *Ask him to send you a list of his safe and unsafe foods. Whatever you do, don't guess. Also ask him to show you what to do if he has a reaction. You, or anyone around him, be they family, friends or work colleagues, should know how to use the adrenaline injection, for example. Have a dry run; then you won't get in a panic if you need to do the real thing. If you are travelling with your friend, then make sure he's told the hotel about his allergies and has asked for an allergen-free meal during the flight.*

Q   **My supermarket doesn't have a 'free-from' list available yet. Where else can I get information?**

A   *Dieticians usually have lists of foods that those with specific food allergies should avoid. These include foods that contain specific and different types of ingredients, which is very useful if the person with the food allergy has to avoid more than one thing. The internet provides this information, as do allergy-related charities, associations and support groups.*

Q   **Do people grow out of their food allergy?**

A   *Some people do. It depends upon the age of the person and the food involved. Most babies will grow out of their allergy to milk, and some children with a proven allergy to peanuts will grow out of it. However, adults with a food allergy, for example to peanuts or shellfish, are more likely to have it for the rest of their lives.*

12

Looking the part

Looking the part (as opposed to looking like a part) is probably the least of your concerns but proper gym wear can make all the difference between a good session and an afternoon in A&E.

Let's get one thing straight from the start — this idea has nothing to do with fashion.

No area of human endeavour has produced more ludicrous outfits than the fitness business (OK, there's ballroom dancing and golf...). A quick look around any gym will reveal at least a couple of lurid skin-tight nightmares that any self-respecting 70s glam rocker would have turned down as too showy. Fashion gets left behind in the locker, but function, ah now that's another story. When it comes to function the choice between good and bad gear can mean the difference between performing at your peak or winding up in hospital. Read on and rate the contents of *your* gym bag.

KEEPING YOUR FEET ON THE GROUND

Shoes are the make-or-break item in your gym bag, but most people choose them on either price or brand without a thought to what they're actually going to do. Most 'sports' shoes have no right to be in a gym because they're completely unsuitable and won't protect you.

Here's an idea for you...

You can get an idea of whether you're a pronator or supinator simply by looking at the underside of your current shoes and checking the wear pattern. Most of us wear down more on one side of the heel than the other. The way they've worn will tell even more to a shoe specialist, so remember to take your old gym shoes with you when you go to the shop to get advice on a new pair.

Running shoes

What could be simpler than left foot, right foot, repeat? Except that the forces on your body when you run are phenomenal. The entire weight of your bounding body comes crashing down on one small part of your foot. It's only common sense to provide padding at that point but it turns out we all run in different ways and one of the key differences is the way our feet take the shock. To the experts that's called pronation.

With a neutral footfall the first point of impact is the heel. Then the sole of the foot is planted, and the force rolls up toward the ball. Finally you spring off your toes. Loading the heel and the ball with shock absorbers looks like good sense. Or would do if any of us had a truly neutral footfall.

Most of us *overpronate* to a certain degree: our foot lands on the outside edge of the heel and rolls inwards as the weight is shifted to the ball and off again. There's nothing wrong with that, but clearly a well-designed shoe for an overpronator will cushion the outside edge of the foot. And just to make things more awkward, some people do just the opposite and *oversupinate* – they roll their feet outwards. As if that wasn't enough some of us have an unusually strong heelstrike, and some of us strike on the ball of the foot. Each different way of running requires a different design of shoe to minimise the impact. If you overpronate or oversupinate a lot you may even need what are called stability shoes to help balance your biomechanics.

So if you just pick up a pair of shoes on the basis of the colour or the logo you will be doing yourself no favours when it comes to the hard impact of running. There will always be someone who hammers away on the treadmill in nothing but a holed pair of green-flash tennis shoes, but as they get older they will also be the experts on overuse injuries, shin splints and knackered knees.

'If you can't fly, then run. If you can't run, then walk. If you can't walk, then crawl. But whatever you do, keep moving.'
MARTIN LUTHER KING, JR

Defining idea...

There's only one answer. Get thee to a specialist running shop where someone can see you run and suggest shoes to suit you. My favourite shop videos your feet as you run and then talks you through the tape. Some shops have treadmills where you can try out shoes, and all of them have a street outside so there's no excuse for them trying to sell you a shoe if they haven't seen you run in it. A proper fit is key to getting fit. Wear the wrong shoes, with the wrong degree of cushioning, and you're increasing the risk of injury.

Cross-trainers
Running shoes are great for running – but running, while very high impact, is just one kind of motion. Unless you're a very unusual runner indeed your feet will always be moving forwards, whereas the moment you indulge in martial arts, step or just about any other training you will start moving sideways, jumping and changing direction suddenly. Now your foot needs lateral cushioning and probably some ankle protection. Enter the cross-trainer. If you fight shy of the treadmill but can't resist those step classes, then you'd do better to get a dedicated cross-trainer. The golden rule is to buy the shoe to suit the job it's going to do, not to suit the suits in the marketing department.

SLICK WICKING

That baggy cotton T-shirt may feel just great, but cotton worn next to the skin is not the best for the roaring gym beastie you are about to become. Work out and you will sweat. Sweat in cotton and your clothes will soon be sporting large, cold, damp patches. For your own comfort and performance, switch to a wicking fabric. Wicking clothes are modern synthetics (careful with them in the wash) that wick sweat away by spreading it rapidly through their fibres where it more readily evaporates. That cools you down in the process. Nike introduced the wicking revolution with a fabric called Dri-Fit but these days every single brand has much the same thing under a different name.

BE IN CONTROL OF THE BOUNCE

Seriously good sports bras are invaluable and for the larger lady that will mean something with a lot more support than a crop top from Sweaty Betty. Try the Less Bounce site (www.lessbounce.co.uk) or SportsBras (www.sportsbras.co.uk).

NO-NOS

No jewellery – please. I don't know how he did it but I can still remember seeing a lad who managed to get his chunky ID bracelet caught in the (moving) seat of the rower he was sitting in. Everyone was so fascinated it was ages before anyone offered to help.

Q   **I went to a specialist running shop and it turns out that I have very wide feet. Is that a problem?**

How did it go?

A   *It can be if you squeeze them into narrow trainers. Even if it doesn't seem uncomfortable your foot will try and bust out through the walls of the trainer which reduces their ability to protect your precious plates of meat. Certain specialist running shoe makers do six widths or more per size. Ask in a good running shop.*

Q   **I've seen people wearing plastic waterproof tops and trousers in the gym to help 'sweat' weight off. Does it work?**

A   *Nope. As well as being plain nasty the 'sweating' weight off approach doesn't get rid of fat. It just makes you lose water. As a result of their extra sweatiness the people in the bin bag outfits will weigh less after the session, but unless they want to be dangerously dehydrated they will have to replace all that lost fluid a.s.a.p. It's true that boxers do it, but that's just to get under a certain weight at the moment of weigh in.*

Q   **Do I need both running shoes and cross-trainers?**

A   *Cross-trainers are all-rounders. If you're serious about running you will need running shoes. If you only venture onto the treadmill for a mile or two a week at a gentle pace, then cross-trainers will do you fine – for now.*

13

On doctor's orders?

The wine industry might try to promote wine as an intrinsic part of a healthy diet, but there is no doubt that the effects of heavy drinking are calamitous. Learn to distinguish the myths from the realities.

Read as much as you like about the subject of wine and health and you won't come across many conclusive opinions.

On an almost weekly basis some new study is published promoting the benefits of wine consumption and is contradicted by another blaming wine for a catalogue of ills.

THE GRIM TRUTH

However much the pro-wine lobby might champion the cause of wine consumption, wine is known to be linked to: liver damage, brain damage, cancer, nerve and muscle wasting, blood disorders, raised blood pressure, strokes, skin infections, psoriasis, infertility and birth defects. Wine consumption can also be blamed for all sorts of collateral damage such as road accidents and domestic violence.

Here's an idea for you...

Try to follow the French habit of only ever drinking wine with a meal. Not only does wine taste better with food; it also means that once the wine has been consumed there is sufficient food to absorb some of it in the stomach (try drinking on an empty stomach and you will get the idea). Also have plenty of water to hand. It never pays to quench your thirst with wine.

Defining idea...

'The cheapness of wine seems to be a cause, not of drunkenness but of sobriety... People are seldom guilty of excess in what is their daily fare... On the contrary, in the countries which either from excessive heat or cold, produce no grapes, and where wine consequently is dear and a rarity drunkenness is a common vice.'
ADAM SMITH

SOBERING, ISN'T IT?

One fact that undermines the case of the pro-wine lobby is that much of the research is sponsored by those who have a vested interest in the continued growth of wine consumption. Yet, aside from the rash claims made by studies published by various universities (many of which happen to be located in winemaking regions such as Bordeaux and Burgundy), there is fairly convincing evidence that moderate wine consumption does have some benefits. Drinking between one and three glasses of wine a day is believed to reduce the chances of cardiovascular disease. Despite technically being toxic, alcohol offers such benefits as controlling the levels of blood cholesterol and blood-clotting proteins.

One of the great planks of the wine–health debate is based on what is known as the 'French paradox' – the discovery made by US documentary makers that, despite a relatively high intake of alcohol, the French were generally much healthier than people in Anglo-Saxon countries where drinking is more moderate. If this is true, then one of the contributory factors – besides the 'Mediterranean diet' high in fresh fruit and olive oil – might be the rate at which alcohol is consumed. The tendency in many northern European countries is to binge, i.e. to concentrate drinking into a relatively short period of time. In France, since wine is an intrinsic part of the gastronomic experience, the rule seems to be 'a little but often'.

There is also an argument that those who see wines as a source of sensual pleasure are likely to drink less wine than those who drink simply to get drunk. The more that free-thinking drinkers immerse themselves in the field of wine appreciation by learning to savour the wonderful flavours and aromas that wine offers, the less they will see wine as a social prop.

'Fermented beverages have been preferred over water throughout the ages: they are safer, provide psychotropic effects, and are more nutritious. Some have even said that alcohol was the primary agent for the development of Western civilisation, since more healthy individuals (even if inebriated for much of the time) lived longer and had greater reproductive success.'
PATRICK McGOVERN

Defining idea...

THE PROBLEM OF CHEAP WINE

A growing problem in recent years that is rarely highlighted is the falling price of wine; the combination of better technology and increased volume of wine being produced has meant that the cost of a bottle has fallen dramatically over the last twenty years. The fact that wine is no longer a luxury and so much more accessible has helped to drive up wine consumption. There is no doubt, too, that cheap wine now tastes much better than it ever did in the past – leaps and bounds in winemaking know-how have created a new generation of fruity inexpensive wines that are dangerously easy to drink.

How did it go?

Q   The French seem to drink wine with every meal. Can that really be a wise habit to adopt?

A   *Yes, many do, but often the quantities consumed are negligible. A glass of wine is treated as part of the gastronomic fundamentals – alongside bread and water, oil and vinegar.*

Q   I'm rather confused. In some respects wine seems to be beneficial. In others it seems incredibly damaging. What are we supposed to believe?

A   *There is no doubt that excessive alcohol consumption has a detrimental effect upon health. If it had been invented in the twentieth century it would almost certainly have been banned. But all studies into health constitute an inexact science. You have to make up your own mind about what you consider safe levels of consumption – and what risks you are prepared to take.*

Q   Are some people more at risk than others?

A   *Yes. What complicates the matter is that alcohol consumption affects us all in different ways. Much depends on our size, gender and metabolism.*

14

For men only

Real men do take care of their health – and even go to the doctor – if they want to live longer.

We all know that men and women were created equal – except, that is, when it comes to living longer.

Women outlive men by nearly six years and the gender gap is getting wider. Doctors think hormones may have a part to play. During their reproductive years, women are much less likely than men to suffer from heart disease, because their high levels of oestrogen lower LDL (bad) cholesterol and raise HDL (good) cholesterol. (After the menopause, when oestrogen levels drop, heart disease becomes the leading cause of death in women as well as men.) It's thought that oestrogen can also help to protect women from stroke and colon cancer.

It's unlikely that men would queue up for artificial doses of oestrogen to help them live longer. But there are many lifestyle changes that you can make that will help you live as long as women. Giving up smoking is the first one – for all the media hype about teenage girls taking up smoking, the biggest group of smokers is still men. Drinking is another concern. Despite all the news coverage about women becoming binge drinkers, heavy drinking – which increases the incidence of hypertension, stroke, liver disease, accidents and various cancers – is still most

Here's an idea for you...

If it's been a while since you saw your doctor, write down a list of all the concerns you'd raise in your ideal, fantasy consultation. Now, choose the most important of these concerns, make an appointment and talk it through thoroughly. You'll get the most out of your appointment if you focus on one problem rather than listing a raft of niggles. Try writing any questions you have before you get there, and make a note of the main symptoms, when they first appeared, and what, if any, medication you've used to treat it in the past.

prevalent in men. (Have you ever walked into a local bar and found it full of solitary female drinkers? Probably not.)

Men also eat fewer vegetables than women. And when overweight, they tend to carry the weight on their stomachs, becoming the classic apple shape, unlike women, who carry it on their hips and thighs. Fat stored in the abdominal region is associated with an increased risk of heart disease.

But perhaps the biggest factor of all is that women take better preventative care of themselves than men. They spend more time finding out about health, and are more likely to notice symptoms and report them to their doctor. According to research, when men finally do get themselves to the doctor, they are more likely to play down their symptoms – and then ignore the advice given.

It's time to abandon the macho mentality that real men don't go to the doctor. If it's the white coat that makes you feel uncomfortable, next time you walk past your surgery, walk in and pick up a leaflet about the services on offer. Most surgeries now offer a team of experts and range of services, so you may be able to get your problem sorted without even seeing a doctor. The practice nurse, for example, can test your blood pressure and cholesterol level or deal with other routine matters, often in a drop-in clinic. Some medical centres also have physiotherapists, counsellors and even specialist 'well man' clinics. Remember, it's your taxes that are funding these services so get out there and make the most of them!

'If you compare all the major killers, such as heart disease and lung cancer, men easily come out best, from the undertaker's point of view.'
DR IAN BANKS, Chairman of the Men's Health Forum

Defining idea...

'Old age is like everything else. To make a success of it, you've got to start young.'
FRED ASTAIRE

Defining idea...

How did it go?

Q **I've been feeling a bit odd recently. Is it true that there's a male menopause?**

A *It's true that levels of the male hormone testosterone decline with age and that at eighty, you'll have half the testosterone you had at twenty. But it's a very slow, steady decline that starts around the age of forty so it shouldn't produce any specific symptoms in the way that the female menopause does. However, some experts believe that levels can drop more rapidly than normal in some men, resulting in symptoms such as fatigue, a low mood, irritability, lack of energy and concentration. You may find you're not performing so well at work – or in the bedroom. Bear in mind that these symptoms can also be caused by lifestyle factors such as being overweight and unfit, drinking too much and having a poor diet. But if you're otherwise pretty healthy, and your symptoms come on suddenly, your best bet is to discuss it with your doctor who may decide you need hormone tests.*

Q **My father had prostate cancer so I make sure I get the right checks. But what else can I do to make sure I don't get it too?**

A *Eat more tomatoes for a start – an antioxidant found in tomatoes, called lycopene, seems to fight off cancer cells in the prostate. Before you rush off and munch your way through a bag of tomatoes, bear in mind that the body cannot absorb lycopene except in the presence of fat. So simply drinking a glass of tomato juice won't help but eating tomato pastes and sauces which contain a little oil will – and that includes ketchup! Alternatively, warm up some tinned plum tomatoes for breakfast and have them on buttered toast, drizzle fresh tomatoes with olive oil in a salad, or mix fresh tomatoes with sun-dried tomatoes in oil. An added bonus could be healthier arteries – men and women with high levels of lycopene in the bloodstream also have healthy arteries.*

15

Boost your immune system

You can't live younger for longer without a strong immune system – it's your private army, fighting off invasion by foreign organisms that can lead to disease.

Here's how to keep your troops in peak condition and help prevent the illnesses we associate with ageing.

Every day, hordes of bugs (bacteria, viruses, parasites and fungi) are doing their best to get inside your body. To a bug, you're a very attractive proposition: a bijou residence offering warmth, safety and food.

Luckily the body has developed a highly effective defence system for keeping these bugs out. Inside you is an army of scavenging white blood cells, constantly roaming the body looking for invaders. If a scavenging cell spots one, then it's immediately transported to the nearest lymph glands (situated in the neck, armpits and groin) and destroyed before it's even had a chance to wave a white flag. (You can feel this brutal elimination process taking place when your lymph glands become swollen.)

A healthy body with a fully functioning immune system sees off potentially dangerous organisms and carcinogens every day. It's even thought that cancer cells grow and are destroyed by the immune system on a regular basis. It's no surprise that a recent study of healthy centenarians found they had one thing in common: a healthy immune system.

Here's an idea for you... Regular massage not only reduces stress and anxiety, it can also boost the immune system by increasing levels of infection-fighting cells. Can't coerce someone into doing it? Don't have the time or spare cash to see a professional? No problem – simply get a tennis ball, lean against a wall and roll the ball around between your back and shoulders and the wall. Try it – you'll be hooked.

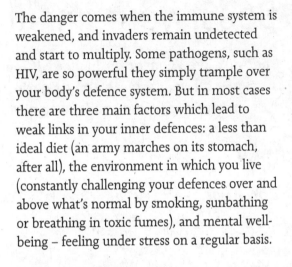

The danger comes when the immune system is weakened, and invaders remain undetected and start to multiply. Some pathogens, such as HIV, are so powerful they simply trample over your body's defence system. But in most cases there are three main factors which lead to weak links in your inner defences: a less than ideal diet (an army marches on its stomach, after all), the environment in which you live (constantly challenging your defences over and above what's normal by smoking, sunbathing or breathing in toxic fumes), and mental well-being – feeling under stress on a regular basis.

YOU ARE WHAT YOU EAT

Your immune system works best when you keep it supplied with a full range of micronutrients such as vitamins and minerals. But even people who eat a balanced diet often show deficiencies and there are two theories about why. When we evolved, we were designed to lead active lives, hunting, gathering and escaping predators, and consuming 3000–4000 calories a day. Now we're mainly sedentary, and need around 2000 calories, we may not be able to eat enough to get the full range of micronutrients we need.

The second theory is that today's intensive farming methods have depleted our soil of key minerals (such as selenium) and our food processing methods further deplete food of micronutrients. We now know that a large number of people are regularly missing out on vitamins A, D and B12; folic acid, riboflavin, iron, magnesium, zinc, copper and omega-3 oils. Plus, nutritionists think we're more likely to have deficiencies as we get older, because the digestive system becomes less efficient at absorbing micronutrients from the food we eat.

So strengthening your immune system starts with taking a good multivitamin and mineral supplement every day. By the way, simply buying the bottle and leaving it in the kitchen drawer doesn't work! You need to top up your micronutrients every day (so a bottle just lasts as long as it says on the label – 30, 60 or 90 days – not all year). This really helps: there was a US study of older people with weakened immune systems. After taking a daily nutritional supplement they had fully functioning immune systems within a year.

BE AWARE OF YOUR ENVIRONMENT

Your body has a regular army designed to fight off everyday invaders, and it also has a troop of 'special forces', called T-cells, held in reserve for extraordinary circumstances. But if you bombard your body with extra invaders on a regular basis, the effectiveness of these special forces is inevitably weakened, allowing disease-causing bugs to multiply. And while you can't control the many bacteria and viruses that assault your immune system every day, you do have control over additional toxic invaders such as cigarette smoke (whether first-hand or passive) and, to a lesser extent, environmental pollution.

THE MIND/BODY FACTOR

Undergoing stress on a regular basis is like offering a personal invitation to foreign invaders to walk through the chinks it causes in your defences. Many of the hormones involved in your body's fight or flight response – how it responds to stress – are actually immune suppressants, slowing down its natural disease-fighting mechanisms. Ever noticed how you're more prone to colds when you feel under pressure? It's not just your imagination. People in one study were most likely to develop a cold if they had experienced a negative life event in the past year. It's also been found that the effectiveness of a pneumonia vaccine was reduced if recipients were suffering from stress.

How did it go?

Q   I cycle to work along a fairly busy route – would driving be better for my immune system?

A   *No; in fact, the opposite is true. The pollution hotspot is in the centre of the road where cars drive. Pollution levels fall dramatically towards the side of the road where cyclists and pedestrians travel. So keep up the cycling!*

Q   What is the easiest way to tell if my immune system needs a boost?

A   *A good indication is how you shake off minor illnesses. Do you get more than two colds a year? Are cuts and grazes slow to heal? If so, you should start supporting your immune system today.*

16

Chemical world

We can't avoid all the man-made chemicals out there. We can, however, choose alternatives for many.

There's no point in getting paranoid. We live in the twenty-first century and there's no going back in time, however much we'd like to! We need to manage the amount of man-made chemicals we draw into our bodies and think of alternatives to those we expose ourselves to daily.

The point is that exposure to low levels of chemicals is relatively harmless. We're surrounded by low-level doses of chemicals, from the fire retardants in our armchairs and mattresses to the toxins in toothpaste and cosmetics. It's the continual exposure to chemicals and the fact that we're so reliant on so many different products that's a worry, say some – the drip, drip, drip. Chemicals are, of course, in everything. Even fruit and vegetables contain chemicals – naturally occurring toxins that protect the plant against attacks by insects, fungi, birds and animals. Day to day these natural chemicals are said to outnumber the man-made ones by a factor of 20,000:1. It has

Reduce the number of chemicals you are exposed by purifying the air that you breathe. Air purifiers are available for the home, the car or even to wear when you are out and about. www.healthy-house.co.uk provides these and all sorts of other gizmos for a healthy environment.

been found that two-thirds of the man-made chemicals are carcinogenic to rats and mice, but so are the natural ones. It seems that although fruit and vegetables might contain toxic elements, they also contain elements that protect us against cancer as well. So, it appears that their toxicity is offset somewhat by the protective factors they provide. Then there's the possibility that we've adapted over millions of years to these natural toxins, whereas we've only been exposed to the man-made ones for the last fifty years or so.

It's tempting to throw the baby out with the bath water forgetting that there have been incidences where chemicals have saved many lives. DDT, for example, helped rid much of the world of the malarial mosquito, although due to its toxicity it's now banned in many countries.

FISH LADY

In the 1960s, some fishermen noticed that something very strange was going on with the fish they caught. Male fish resembled female fish and this led to the discovery of environmental oestrogens (xeno-oestrogens). It's unlikely you'll turn into a fish or from a man into a woman from such low exposure, but it's worth avoiding these sources of xeno-oestrogens wherever possible. Soft plastics are a source, like the plastic wraps for food – it's therefore best to keep cheese in hard, airtight plastic or ceramic containers than wrapped in something like clingfilm. And it isn't good to leave plastic water bottles lying in the sun either.

A QUICK TOUR OF THE NASTIES!

So, what do we mean by man-made chemicals and what do they purportedly do to us?

- **PCBs** (polychlorinated biphenyls) – chemicals that can affect the functioning of the thyroid. They were mainly used as paint additives until they were banned in the 70s, but recent reports show high levels in oily fish.

- **Phthalates** – used to make plastics more flexible, including in children's toys. They're also found in cosmetics. Lab tests have shown that these chemicals affect sperm count and quality.

- **Organotins** – toxic even in small quantities, but are nevertheless found in trainers, mattresses, bed linen, upholstered furniture, carpets and floor coverings. These chemicals are known to affect the immune system.

- **Bisphenol A** – found in cosmetics.

- **Tricolosan** –an antibiotic used in some plastic cutting boards and in mouthwashes, detergents, creams and lotions. This chemical is stored in the body for long periods.

'The more clearly we can focus our attention on the wonders and realities of the universe about us, the less taste we shall have for destruction.'
RACHEL CARSON, author of *Silent Spring*, one of the first books that exposed the possible dangers of modern chemicals

Defining idea...

How did
it go?

Q   This no chemical stuff is all very well, but I don't find the natural alternatives very effective.

A   *You could try Ecover (www.store.ediblenature.com) for a wonderful selection of nature-friendly products to use in the home. I find them very efficient and changed over to their fabulous washing powder years ago. A network marketing company that has a good reputation for cleaning products is Neways (www.neways.com).*

Q   What about cleaning my face? Are there any good products out there?

A   *I use either Dr Hauschka, which is delicious and apparently used by all the top supermodels (www.drhauschka.co.uk), or Jurlique, an Australian company that uses organic and bio-dynamically grown herbs without the use of petro-or coal tar chemicals in their products (www.jurlique.com.au).*

Q   How can I stop myself from coming into contact with man-made chemicals?

A   *You can't, so stop worrying about it. The trick is not to overexpose yourself to them. If you're cleaning the bathroom with domestic chemicals, make sure the area is well ventilated – open the door and windows and breathe away from the products. After years of being exposed to cleaning fluids, my cleaner is now almost completely allergic to any chemical products, suffering from symptoms such as watering eyes and sneezing. She either has to wear a mask or use natural, non-toxic products. So, avoiding a situation like this before it arises is key!*

17

Cellulite busting

The exercise moves, the creams, the treatments, the foods, the pants – one way or another, you *will* beat cellulite.

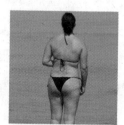

Cellulite is a reminder that life can be cruel. It afflicts nearly 85% of women – including supermodels. (Okay, so it's not always that cruel!)

Strangely, though, men don't notice cellulite. Apparently, if they get that close to naked flesh, they honestly don't care what kind of minor imperfections greet them.

Still, that's no comfort to the millions of women who suffer with cellulite. We hate it! And it's bloody hard to shift.

Cellulite, in case you need an explanation, is that lumpy dimply skin we get on our bottoms, thighs, tummies and even arms. Over the years, many a column inch has been devoted to theories on what it could be. Now the consensus is that it's fat. And the reason why men don't get it is that women's fat cells are shaped differently; the connective fibres that keep the fat in place run horizontally in women, diagonally in men. So, if women's fat cells become enlarged, they tend to

Here's an
idea for
you...

A DIY massage is a good night-time treatment. Gently but firmly massage your legs and thighs using upward movements in a gentle kneading motion, always working towards your heart.

squish upwards and poke out of the top, like squashing butter through cheesecloth, hence its appearance.

There are countless reasons for this. Being overweight is one. Water retention plays a part, as these fat cells have more fluid in them than other cells. This is often the result of a sedentary lifestyle that has caused your circulation and lymphatic drainage system to slow down. This means that your skin doesn't get the vital supply of blood and oxygen required to nourish it, and you retain fluid, which makes those bulges worse. Various bad habits, from smoking to too much booze or a poor diet, can cause free radical damage. Free radicals are nasty destructive forces that attack our skin's collagen and make our skin tissues weaker, which means they lose their lovely youthful elasticity.

Fortunately, there are steps you can take:

EXERCISE MORE

Research has shown that women who followed a low-fat diet and did twenty minutes of aerobic exercise weekly, including some strength exercises, lost 3.5 kg in weight (nearly 5 cm from their thighs). Plus 70% of women said that their cellulite improved in just six weeks by doing weight training aimed at their legs.

When you exercise you boost your circulation and lymph drainage, so you build muscle that effectively boosts the skin, which helps flatten out those bumpy bits. Plus, taking more exercise – at least twenty to thirty minutes three to five times a week – can help shift some of the fat that causes cellulite.

Aim to do three sessions a week of aerobic exercise such as cycling, running, dancing, kickboxing or a fitness video. Also, make sure you're doing some resistance or strength work as building lean muscle is vital; good moves are lunges, squats or 'step' work (cycle uphill, try a step class or run on a treadmill at an incline).

'If I had been around when Rubens was painting, I would have been revered as a fabulous model. Kate Moss? Well, she would have been the paintbrush.'
DAWN FRENCH

Defining idea...

WATCH YOUR DIET

Losing a few pounds can help reduce the fat that causes your cellulite. Try to cut back on salt, which causes water retention, and on fatty and sugary foods. Eat tons of fruit and vegetables, as these are rich in antioxidants that help mop up the free radicals that can damage skin and cause wrinkles and sagging. Also eat plenty of potassium-rich foods such as carrots, broccoli and watermelon to help balance your body's fluid levels, and fish, which contains fatty acids that are good for healthy skin.

Aim to drink about 2 litres of water a day to help boost circulation and reduce water retention. And watch your alcohol and coffee intake, as both can interfere with your circulation.

BODY BRUSH AND PAMPER

Tons of treatments involve algae, body wraps and machine-based pummelling to help fight cellulite. They aim to help boost the skin's circulation, reduce water retention and soften and condition the skin. Try them, but don't expect miracles.

'The chief excitement in a woman's life is spotting women who are fatter than she is.'
HELEN ROWLAND, writer

Endermologie is arguably the only salon treatment that has any proven results. You'll need about ten sessions and a healthy bank account to see the results for yourself, but it could be worth a try. It's a deep-tissue massage treatment using a machine that rolls back and forth across your cellulite to break down fat cells and firm your skin. It comes from France, where they take cellulite very seriously (have you ever seen a French woman with cellulite?), and is approved in the US by the FDA as an effective, albeit temporary, treatment for cellulite.

A cheaper option is to body brush every day. Body brushing is thought to help boost the skin's circulation and lymph flow, which can help beat the fluid build that swells your fat cells. It's also softening because it exfoliates the dead skin that accumulates on the surface.

Start at your feet and with a brush made from natural fibres brush in long strokes (always in the direction of your heart). Ideally do it morning and night before a shower or bath.

Cellulite tends to look worse on dry or dehydrated skin, so moisturising can help minimise its appearance. Experiment with anti-cellulite beauty creams, too. All will probably help moisturise your skin and improve its texture; some may also contain ingredients to help improve circulation, reduce fluid retention and boost production of collagen. Again, use alongside a healthy low-fat diet and regular exercise; miracles haven't been bottled quite yet.

Q **Can you recommend any great exercises that target thighs and bottoms?**

A *Try the donkey kick. Get on all fours, with your hands under your shoulders and your knees in line with your hips. Drop down on to your forearms, keeping your back straight and tummy muscles tight. Now kick the left leg up, keeping the bend in the leg so the upper part of the leg becomes horizontal. Keep the foot flexed, return the leg to the ground and repeat ten to twenty times on that leg. Then kick the right leg up and repeat the process. Build up to three sessions on each leg.*

Q **I've heard about cellulite-eating pants. Are they for real?**

A *I don't know about the eating part, but yes there are seam-free pants designed to sculpt and define your hips and bottom thanks to the compression action and 'micro-massage'. In one study, women who wore LipoShape (www.liposhape.co.uk) pants for twelve hours a day for eight weeks reduced their hips by up to 7 cm, their thighs by 3 cm and their bottoms by 3 cm.*

How did it go?

18

Mattress matters

Is your bed soft or lumpy? Have you had it for over fifteen years? It may be time to look for a new one.

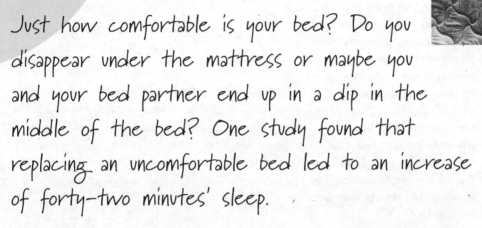

Just how comfortable is your bed? Do you disappear under the mattress or maybe you and your bed partner end up in a dip in the middle of the bed? One study found that replacing an uncomfortable bed led to an increase of forty-two minutes' sleep.

Did you know that beds should be replaced every eight to ten years, by which time they've deteriorated by as much as 75% – yet the average couple hang on to their haven of slumber for fifteen years or more? This can not only lead to back pain, it can mean you're tossing and turning all night trying to get into a comfortable position. The result? You wake up in the night, you don't sleep so soundly, your sleep time is cut short and you feel groggy the next day.

To relieve and prevent back pain you need a bed with the correct support and comfort. The idea is to keep your spine in correct alignment, while the bed moulds

Here's an idea for you...

Go into a shop with a list of your priorities and concerns in advance – health, size, storage, price and so on. There are so many different types of bed that you could be tempted by something you don't really need. Narrow your choice down to two or three and then spend plenty of time – with your partner if you have one – lying on these in your normal sleeping positions. Five or ten minutes should be the minimum for each bed – but feel free to spend half an hour, though any longer and you'll be in danger of settling down for the night.

itself to your natural body contours. This will also mean you'll be moving around less, too. Remember, you're going to spend over 29,000 hours on your bed during an average lifespan so it's worth taking a little time and effort to make the right choice.

BEFORE YOU BUY ...

- Consider a bigger bed. People just don't buy large enough beds. Three-quarters of all double beds are still the standard 4ft 6in x 6ft 3in (135 x 190cm) – yet this is plainly not room enough for two adults to sleep comfortably together without disturbing each other. Studies have shown that couples sleep better in a bigger bed – on average we prod each other 120 times a night. No wonder the Victorians favoured separate bedrooms. If that's not an option, go for size. The standard is still the most popular size, but over a quarter of us opt for bigger beds. Even upgrading to the next size, a 5ft/150cm king size, whilst it takes up very little extra bedroom space, makes a considerable difference! Most shops now have 6ft (180cm) beds too.

- Look for a supportive rather than a hard bed – gone are the days when people thought you needed a hard bed for a good night's sleep. The modern view is that correct support (which is dependent on your weight and build) coupled with comfort is best. Don't automatically go for an orthopaedic bed either – often a medium firm bed with proper cushioning is better.

- Look at pocket spring beds – they tend to feel softer, as they are packed with more upholstery and also feature smaller, lighter springs than a conventional mattress. Because they have so many springs packed tightly together, they give good individual support.

- Consider a waterbed. Forget 70s sex comedies; waterbeds can seriously improve your sleep. Just lying on a waterbed is a relaxing experience – it's like floating and you get a feeling of weightlessness. Most waterbeds have a heater, so you can choose a temperature to suit you. They also conform perfectly to your body, so you're less likely to move around.

- Get a space bed – well, a foam mattress based on NASA technology. The mattress stops tossing and turning by moulding to the shape and position of your body. On an uncomfortable bed, your body needs to change position because of unrelieved pressure. Your blood flow is restricted and there's a build up of pressure – this makes you uncomfortable and forces your body to reposition. When your spine is supported in the correct anatomical shape, there's less pressure build up and therefore less tossing and turning.

'My dream would be to work from my bed – a big bed with eternally fresh sheets – so that I could doze off whenever I wanted to and work in between.'
ANNA RAEBURN

Defining idea…

How did it go?

Q   When should I buy a new bed?

A   *Don't wait until your bed is uncomfortable or damaged before replacing it, by which time your sleep quality could be quite severely affected – use other triggers. Even a good-quality bed will only last around ten years.*

Q   I want to buy a pocket spring mattress but the ones I have seen seem lumpy. Will it be comfortable?

A   *Yes. Luxury, pocket spring beds don't have flat surfaces – they mould themselves to your body shape and the indentation remains even if you turn the bed regularly.*

Q   What kind of pillow should I look for?

A   *Choose a pillow which supports your neck and make sure it lines up with the rest of the spine. Too many pillows thrust the head forward or sideways (depending on your sleeping position) which can create a crick in the neck.*

19

What's your poison?

A cigarette contains over 400 toxic chemicals. Line up for your deadly dose of poisons and see just what goes inside your body every time you light up.

Question: What do nylon, embalming fluid, paint stripper, weed killer, mirrors and plastic all have in common?

Answer: They all use ingredients that you smoke in your cigarette.

Lots of people love the thrill of drinking cocktails – the exotic blend of ingredients, the colour and sparkle of the end product when it's brought to your table. You can choose from a menu showing exactly what's going into the drink and gain some idea of what it will taste like.

On a more mundane level, when we go to the supermarket we can pick up a packet or a bottle and read what's gone into a product before we buy. We can avoid monosodium glutamate or saturated fats, aspartame sweetener or peanuts.

Here's an idea for you...

Write a list of what is bad about smoking. Photocopy it and pin it up in every room in the house and at work, so that you're constantly reminded.

How come when we buy our packet of cigarettes all we know is that we're buying tobacco, with a warning that SMOKING KILLS? No list of ingredients to be seen. So what is in a cigarette? Most of us can roll out the three most obvious

Nicotine is a substance found naturally in the tobacco plant. It is, however, also a deadly poison. It takes only seven seconds from inhaling for nicotine to be absorbed into your bloodstream and reach your brain. That's twice as efficient as injecting it into your arm. Nicotine is also highly addictive – more addictive, in fact, than heroin.

Tar is produced as a result of the manufacturing process of cigarettes. You ingest this directly into your lungs when you smoke and it builds up a coating on the alveoli (mini-branches within the lungs) that reduces your ability to absorb life-giving oxygen.

Carbon monoxide is what comes out of car exhausts and your cigarette. In high concentrations it's highly toxic – suicide by cigarettes just takes longer. Carbon monoxide binds avidly to haemoglobin (in red blood cells) in your bloodstream, thereby preventing the uptake of oxygen. Smokers generally have 10–15% less oxygen in their bloodstream than non-smokers. You need the oxygen to power your muscles, so the heart has to pump extra hard to provide it.

These are the main players, but cigarettes give you a whole lot more!

LET'S HEAR IT FOR CANCER

Cigarettes deliver a positive cornucopia of cancer-inducing chemicals (carcinogens), including the following.

Benzene causes dizziness and light-headedness, irritates the nose and throat, and may cause an upset stomach and vomiting. It's used as a solvent for gums, fats, waxes and resins, in the manufacture of drugs and the production of nylon, as well as being found in petrol.

Formaldehyde is a highly flammable liquid/gas, used as a disinfectant, germicide, fungicide and embalming fluid, and in home insulation and pressed wood products. It irritates the eyes, nose and throat, and can cause skin and lung allergy.

Selenium increases the risk of lung cancer if consumed in large quantities through smoking. In modest amounts (in nutritional supplements, for example) it's an essential micromineral and an antioxidant. Cigarettes are not a nutritional supplement.

Beryllium causes severe bronchitis or pneumonia after high exposure, and can permanently scar the lungs and other body organs. It's used widely in manufacturing electrical components, chemicals, ceramics and X-ray tubes.

Cadmium can cause malformations in a foetus and reproductive damage, as well as permanent kidney damage, emphysema, anaemia and loss of the sense of smell.

'R.J. Reynolds does not – and will not – use any cigarette ingredient if scientific evaluations indicate that it will increase the inherent toxicity of tobacco smoke.'
R.J. Reynolds Industries website, 2005

Defining idea...

83

Defining idea...

'Some ingredients may be added to tobacco during manufacture for various reasons. It is our policy to assess the appropriateness and acceptability of all ingredients prior to use.'
Imperial Tobacco website, 2005

Nickel may damage the developing foetus, as well as causing coughing, shortness of breath and fluid in the lungs. It is used in electroplating and in making coins, batteries, catalysts and metal alloys such as stainless steel.

[Not to mention polycyclic hydrocarbons, nitrosamines, beta-naphthylamine and 4-aminobiphenil.]

Okay, so now you've set up the ideal conditions for a cancer to start growing (take your pick – lung, mouth, throat, larynx, bladder, cervix etc.). What you need now are some chemicals to help it on its way. Guess what? Cigarettes provide these too. And while we're there, let's throw in a few other toxins for good measure.

ALSO STARRING

Ammonia, used in making fertilisers, plastics, dyes and textiles, is produced by rotting and decomposing animal and vegetable matter. It can irritate the lungs, causing coughing and/or shortness of breath, and can lead to a fatal build-up of fluid in the lungs (pulmonary oedema).

Acetone is an ingredient in most paint strippers and varnish removers. It can make you dizzy and light-headed, and can irritate your eyes, nose and throat.

Hydrogen cyanide is extremely poisonous and can irritate the skin, causing a rash.

Arsenic is a poison often used in insecticides and weed killers (and Victorian murders). Very handy for making some military poison gases.

Lead can cause tiredness, mood changes, headaches, stomach problems and insomnia, and increases the risk of high blood pressure.

Mercury is used in thermometers, barometers, vapour lamps, mirror coating, and in making chemicals and electrical equipment. It's highly corrosive.

[Not to mention cresol, phenol, acrolein (from the burning paper), nitric oxide and nitrogen dioxide.]

How did
it go?

Q **If cigarettes have all this rubbish in them, how come they don't taste foul?**

A *Tobacco manufacturers add ingredients like sugar, liquorice, chocolate, herbs and spices to improve the taste.*

Q **You're kidding. You're just trying to scare me. How can something so dangerous still be legal?**

A *Good question. If someone tried to introduce cigarettes onto the market today they'd be thrown out on their ear. Too many powerful interests are involved, that's why. Big multinationals, governments and lots and lots of profit. Believe me, everything written above is true. If anyone tells you different, they either work for a tobacco company, own shares in one or are a politician.*

20

Kick-start your exercise

**Physical exercise is the antidote to pressures in your life.
So muscle into the local walking group, dip into swimming,
tire yourself out cycling...**

Regular exercise will make you feel
better and lift your mood. It'll drop your
cholesterol, help prevent your blood clotting, stop
high blood pressure from developing and help you
maintain a healthy weight.

And, if that's not enough to motivate you: a third and more of coronary heart
disease is due to inactivity...

So gradually increase the amount of exercise you do each day. Take your time
building up your muscles and ligaments to increase your fitness and their strength.
Work towards doing thirty minutes of moderate intensity activity on at least five
days a week. The thirty minutes can be accumulated throughout the day in ten- to
fifteen-minute bouts. 'Moderate intensity' means breathing slightly harder than
normal but staying within your comfort zone. Extend some of your exercise
sessions to forty-five minutes or more. This will encourage your body to use some of

Here's an idea for you...

Know your calorie equivalents to exercise. Different types of exercise burn calories at various rates. Cycling at 16 kilometres or 10 miles an hour, for one hour, burns 240 calories. If you pedal really fast at an average 17 mph you'll burn 720 calories in an hour. Walking 5 km in an hour burns off 260 calories; running 9 km in an hour is equivalent to 600 calories. Cross-country skiing really devours calories – 1400 per hour. Compare these to just standing about, when you'll burn a mere 100 calories an hour.

Defining idea...

'Every day, in every way, I am getting better and better.'
ÉMILE COUÉ, French psychotherapist

your fat stores as a source of energy. We're not all born-again athletes. But we can all integrate exercise into our day, however busy we are. Here's how. Start when you get up in the morning. No, not with a 'Jane Fonda' type of workout, unless you want to, but more of a marching on the spot while you brush your teeth, or loosening your shoulders and stretching your limbs when drying off after your morning shower or as you get dressed. Exercise your pelvic floor or move your lumbar spine around when sitting in the car or on the bus or tube. Squeeze in various muscle groups and hold for the count of ten. Here are some more ideas.

- Walk up and down stairs, pointedly avoiding the lift or escalator. All the better if you're carrying heavy bags – that's extra exercise without you realising it, except the huffing and puffing and sweat lines on your clothes are a bit of a giveaway. And start campaigning for extra provision for bicycles: then capture some of the energy you put into that campaign for when you're actually cycling!

- Get up from your desk little and often. Take frequent trips to the printer and photocopier. Do exercises while you're waiting for a printout or the kettle to boil – maybe some dance steps if no one's looking…

  'My heart is in my boots.'
  BORIS JOHNSON, UK politician

  Defining idea…

- Remember when people actually took a lunch break? Well, get out the staff charter, if you have one, rediscover your entitlement, and get out there – for a walk, a quick swim or cycle ride. Go for a purpose if that helps, perhaps to post a letter, buy your sandwiches or debrief with a friend.

- Do some exercise when you're watching TV – don't just sit there, slumped, doing an imitation of a corpse. Pause the video and take a walking break. A quick spin on your exercise bike or ten sit-ups, while watching your programme or in the commercial break, and you've done some of your exercise stint for the day.

- Do your own housework or gardening; treasure the opportunity to work off those calories or strengthen your muscles. Spend the money you've saved on domestic help on gym membership or new running shoes.

- Rediscover dancing. Insure your feet, if you're a beginner, against breakages. Take plenty of plasters for all those blisters.

Any exercise helps. If you're on the move and it's keeping you warm, then it's good for you. The best activities for boosting your weight loss and fitness are those involving large muscle groups. These are mainly aerobic exercises: walking, running, swimming or cycling.

How did it go?

Q   I'm keen on weightlifting. Could lifting those heavy weights put too much strain on my heart muscles?

A   *The thing about weightlifting is that you take a big breath and hold it – and, all told, this exercise puts your blood pressure up which is bad for your heart. Lift a lesser weight many times, rather than a heavy weight less frequently.*

Q   What's the best form of exercise for someone who's really overweight like me?

A   *One of the few advantages of being overweight is that you use more energy when you're walking than a slimmer person does. You won't carry on with regular exercise unless you enjoy doing it, though – or unless you're a masochist. So go for exercise that fits your lifestyle, and one you like doing. When exercise is a pleasure, fitness is easy.*

Q   How can you prioritise yourself over the kids after you've been out at work all day and not seen much of them?

A   *It's never too early to teach your children good habits and ensure that they're active too. Can you exercise together more, having fun as a family? For example, you could swim while the children have their swimming lessons. Choose activity holidays which can involve you all; use the gym at times when all ages are welcome or go to one where there's a crèche.*

21

Keeping abreast

Going for a walk every day could be the best thing you do for the health of your breasts.

Exercise is something we all intend to do — tomorrow. A busy life has a habit of getting in the way of exercising. But if you want that life to continue as long as possible, you've got to make room for some exercise.

Whatever it takes – throwing away the TV, getting up half an hour earlier, giving up ironing clothes – your number one priority to yourself, if you want to be healthy for longer, is to exercise regularly.

Women tend to associate exercise with being skinny, so once you've hit thirty and realised that the key to a happy life is not fitting into a smaller-sized dress, it's easy to ditch the gym along with the fad diets. But the truth is that as you get older exercise gets even more vital. Done on a regular basis, it's one of the most effective ways of staving off breast cancer, the most common cancer in women.

Here's an idea for you...

Why not sign up for a charity fun-run? There are hundreds of women-only walking or running races held in aid of breast cancer research every year. It's a definite win–win situation – you'll reduce your chances of getting breast cancer by training for the race and you'll help to raise funds for research into the bargain.

Let's have some good news – deaths from breast cancer have fallen by 20% over the past decade. But it still affects around one in nine women at some point and your chances of getting it increase with age. But just half an hour of brisk walking a day can reduce your risk by up to 30%. It used to be thought that only intense exercise such as jogging or aerobics decreased the risk, but now the latest research suggests that moderate activities such as walking, cycling or swimming also count. Even a couple of brisk walks a week will make a big difference.

But you'll only benefit from this effect if you're not overweight. It's thought that excess weight increases levels of hormones and growth factors (like oestrogen and insulin) that promote cancer development and that exercise can't counter these effects. But that's no reason to throw away your trainers if you know you need to lose some flab. Doing around thirty minutes of moderate exercise daily will help you lose weight and keep it off. Combine that with a diet high in plant foods – vegetables, fruits, wholegrains, pulses – and moderate amounts of oily fish, and low amounts of meat and saturated fat, and you could further reduce your risk by up to 33%.

And a word of warning. The link between drinking and breast cancer makes sobering reading. One glass a day is fine and if you choose a dark red wine, you'll be getting an antioxidant boost into the bargain. But regularly drinking more than two units of alcohol a day can increase your risk of breast cancer by 40%. It's thought that alcohol interferes with the enzymes that break down oestrogen. If girls' nights out on the town are a thing of the past, it can be easy to assume your drinking is fine. But you also need to keep track of those generous glasses of wine you pour at home. One glass of most wines is around a unit, but that's a 125 ml wine glass. Try to stick to no more than two glasses a night, and have two alcohol-free nights a week. If this doesn't sound like much fun, then think of it another way. If you cut back on quantity you can afford to upgrade the quality – and savour every delicious drop.

'The secret to staying young is to live honestly, eat slowly, and lie about your age.'
LUCILLE BALL

Defining idea...

93

How did it go?

Q **I'm now inspired to check my breasts regularly. What's the best routine?**

A *Doctors have moved on and now no longer recommend a specific routine for breast checking. Instead, they encourage you to simply get to know your breasts. Which may sound a bit odd – but they're not expecting you to look down and say, 'Hi, how do you do?' It's about giving some attention to an area of your body you may take for granted. Which is why you should get your partner in on the act. Both of you should be aware of any changes, rather than just lumps. Any kind of thickening of the breast, change in shape or size, dimpling or puckering of the skin, or a change in the appearance of a nipple should be checked out with your doctor.*

Q **My mum has just been diagnosed with breast cancer. Does that mean I'll get it?**

A *Not at all. Only 4% of breast cancer cases are thought to be genetically linked. The rest are caused by lifestyle factors – which is something you can do something about. But a very small number of women are at especially high risk because of faulty genes known as BRCA1 and BRCA2. If other family members have developed the disease, especially before the age of fifty, see your doctor.*

Q **Is it possible for men to get breast cancer?**

A *Yes, it is, although it's rare. Each year, there are around 200–300 cases of male breast cancer in the UK. This compares with about 40,500 cases of female breast cancer. The same rules apply about being aware of changes in the chest area and reporting them to your doctor.*

22

Walk the walk

Walking is the simplest way to improve your fitness level and fend off the ageing process.

It's easy to incorporate walking into everyday routines, so it's the exercise you're most likely to do consistently and stick at.

Want to add years to your life in an instant? Walk! The great thing about physical activity is that its anti-ageing effects are immediate. So no matter how unfit you've been in the past, if you start exercising now you will live a longer and healthier life. But you've got to do it consistently, and you've got to keep it up. (Don't think you can rest on past athletic laurels – no matter how fit you were once, after five years of being sedentary, you have the same fitness – and body age – as someone who's never exercised at all.) This is why walking is such a great anti-ageing exercise choice.

At this point, you're probably thinking one of two things: walking isn't real exercise, and that you do a lot of walking anyway and you're still not fit. Well, brisk walking – the pace you'd go if you were late for an important appointment – raises your heart rate to between 60–80% of its maximum, the level of activity necessary for strengthening the heart and lungs. But it does so without putting undue strain on your joints – in fact, it can help strengthen bones and stave off osteoporosis. Regular walking will also reduce your risk of heart disease, stroke, diabetes, high

Here's an idea for you...

Want an easy way to keep track of your walking to make sure you're doing enough to stave off ageing? Buy a pedometer or step counter, a cheap little gadget that you wear on your waistband to count every step you take. Aim for 10,000 steps a day (roughly equivalent to five miles). Experts say that's the minimum you need to do to encourage weight loss and bring with it the many anti-ageing benefits associated with lower body fat. But that doesn't mean setting out on a daily hike – every step you take throughout the day counts, be it indoors or out, fast or slow.

blood pressure, bowel cancer and arthritis – as well as psychological conditions such as anxiety, stress and depression. Now studies have shown that regular walking is also good for the brain and can help stave off Alzheimer's. It can also help you lose weight – one study tracked a group of walkers who did a two-mile, hilly route, three times a week. They lost an average of 6.5 kg (14 lb) in three months – without dieting.

Think you already do a lot of walking and aren't fit? You won't get results by walking the kids to school if you go at snail's pace. You should feel warm, sweaty and slightly breathless. Ideally, you should schedule some walking sessions three to five times a week, and work up to doing an hour at a time. On other days, try to fit in three ten-minute walks throughout the day.

For best results, invest in a good pair of trainers and wear comfortable clothing – it doesn't need to be sports kit. Dress in layers – for example a T-shirt, then a sweatshirt which you can take off and tie round your waist when you warm up. A lightweight running jacket is a good investment as it keeps out rain and wind without weighing you down.

Always warm up with five minutes of easy walking before picking up the pace. Then cool down with five minutes of easy walking at the end, and do some stretches. During your walk, keep your tummy muscles pulled in tight to support your back. Think 'tall' – don't slump into your hips. Relax your shoulders and let your arms swing naturally by your sides. Use your natural stride – don't try to lengthen it – and strike the ground with the heel first, rolling through the foot then pushing off with the toe.

'How do you live a long life? Take a two-mile walk every morning before breakfast.'
HARRY S. TRUMAN

Defining idea...

Complete beginners should start with short bursts of walking interspersed with rest periods. Try walking briskly for five minutes, walking slowly (or completely resting) for three, then walking briskly for five. Do this three times a week for two weeks, then start to add a minute a week to the brisk walking bursts. When you feel your fitness improve, begin cutting back on the rest periods. Your aim is to walk briskly for thirty minutes.

Still not convinced it'll get results? When one of the world's most respected anti-ageing scientists, Professor Jay Olshansky of the University of Illinois at Chicago, was asked which single product people should buy to stave off ageing, he replied 'a good pair of walking shoes'.

How did
it go?

Q   I've been walking on a treadmill. Is this as good as walking outside?

A   *It's an excellent start and treadmill walking can be invaluable if it's too cold
or dark to walk outside. But do try to fit in a few daytime walks outdoors
every week. You'll work harder, for a start – constantly changing terrain is
more challenging to the body and you have to work against wind resistance.
Plus, spending time outdoors boosts your mental well-being and helps fend
off depression. In the meantime, get the most out of your treadmill
sessions by setting it to a hill programme to keep your muscles – and your
brain – challenged.*

**Q   I've been wearing a pedometer but some days I'm falling short of
10,000 steps. Any suggestions?**

A   *Plenty! How about pacing around while on the phone; losing your TV remote
control so you have to get up to change channels, walking all (or part) of
the way to work, walking – not riding – up every escalator. (If you can't
walk all the way up an escalator, stand half the way and start walking
towards the top. Try to walk more steps each time.) How about getting your
lunchtime sandwich from a shop half a mile away, offering to walk your
neighbour's dog on a regular basis, walking around the block after dinner in
the evening or planning a long walk into every weekend?*

23

Labelling matters

Have you ever looked at the back of a packet of food and wondered where the actual food was?

The list of ingredients on some packet foods make them look like Martian fodder. Indeed many of the weird and wonderful names certainly aren't things you'd ever use in your home cooking.

Food manufacturers now seem to prefer these long names to the ubiquitous E numbers, as increasingly consumers are realising that E stands for additives.

Food labelling can be hugely confusing. The general rule of thumb is that if the ingredient list barely fits on the back of the packet, put it back on the shelf where you found it. The second rule is that you should recognise the main ingredient and if you don't, or it's something like sugar, reassess your choice. The words 'junk food' should spring to mind.

Here's an idea for you...

Try reading the back of food packets for a week. Don't use items where ingredients aren't in plain English. Watch out especially for hydrogenated fats, which may be cunningly listed as 'shortening'. This is particularly found in cakes, biscuits, margarine and ready meals.

BEWARE THE SUGAR MONSTER!

Sugar is really one to watch as it morphs into all sorts of disguises – glucose, fructose, lactose or maltose and, of course, there's always honey. Watch out too for other forms of sugar like sorbitol, xylitol, mannitol and isomalt. The one that's really crept in is the high fructose corn syrups (sugar dextrose), which isn't the same type of sugar as you find in fruit but is extracted from processing cornstarch to yield glucose. It's much cheaper and sweeter than sugar and is, of course, a firm favourite with food manufacturers – sauces, chewing gum, fruit drinks, canned fruits, dairy products, jams, sweets, bread, bacon and beer are favourite hiding places. Unfortunately, although it may be convenient for the food manufacturers, our bodies struggle to use it as effective fuel and it is easily metabolised as fat. And just as you thought we'd finished with sugar, guess what? There are a whole lot more forms of it, including aspartame (E951), which is 180 times sweeter than sugar. The key ingredients to this are aspartic acid, phenylalanine and methanol, and although the first two are amino acids (protein building blocks) they're not found in this combination in nature.

HOLD BACK ON THE SALT SHAKER

Salt (sodium chloride) is added in generous amounts to processed foods and although we're meant to have a maximum of 6g a day (UK guidelines), you can easily exceed this amount if you don't read the labels. Incidentally, if you're adding a lot of salt to your food, check your nutrient status because you could be short of zinc. A zinc deficiency can stop your taste buds from performing so well.

'Food is one of life's great pleasures. Shopping for it, preparing and eating it has bound people together for centuries. It is in eating together that we are socialised. In the end it's about what kind of society we want.'
FELICITY LAWRENCE, author of *Not on the Label*, an exposé of the food industry

Defining idea...

One good bit of news – a little butter probably beats its synthetic cousin margarine if it contains hydrogenated fats. Fats in this form are very similar to Tupperware, molecularly speaking.

HOW IS YOUR ADDITION?

Food additives are all used for a reason, but there are doubts about their safety. Certainly E284, boric acid, has been linked with causing confusion and, interestingly, is also used to eliminate cockroaches and ants. E321, butylated hydroxytoluene (BHT), has been shown to cause haemorrhaging in animals, while E220, sulphur dioxide, (preservative) can interfere with nutrient absorption and can provoke tingling or flushing. Also, monosodium glutamate (MSG), that favourite additive of Chinese restaurants, is a flavour enhancer that can cause problems in those with sensitivities to it, including headaches and even seizures. But scientists are still undecided about how much of an effect these chemicals exert.

How did it go?

Q **I always go for the low-fat options as I'm quite health conscious. Yoghurts are my particular favourite. Are these OK?**

A *Although the yoghurt may be low fat, it might be high in sugar – some small single-portion yoghurts contain at least four teaspoons of the stuff. Another ingredient to watch out for in yoghurts is modified starch, which is derived from corn and used as a cheap filling agent and thickener. It attracts water, thus adding bulk. Further, to make your banana yoghurt yellow, colourings are often added. And just one more thing to watch out for – if it's labelled 'strawberry yoghurt' it must have some real fruit content, but if it says 'strawberry-flavoured yoghurt' you have just entered synthetic city.*

Q **Although my little boy has a lovely nature, sometimes he goes nuts, gets agitated, rude and can't sit still. Is it something he's eating or am I imagining food can have this effect?**

A *It's probably not your imagination at all. E102, tartrazine, has been linked with hyperactivity in children and it's found in orange colourings.*

24

Could you have diabetes?

Diabetes is increasing on a global scale. Even more concerning is the fact that you could be a sufferer without knowing it. Here's what is has to do with diet and activity levels.

Diabetes is a chronic and incurable disease with nasty complications, such as blindness, kidney failure, stroke and nerve damage.

Diabetes is not new – in the seventeenth century it was called the 'pissing evil' – but it is on the increase. There are two types of diabetes. Type 1 is more commonly found in children and young adults and is treated with a strict diet and insulin injections. It's Type 2 that is on the increase and is strongly linked to obesity and a lack of activity. There are other risk factors over which we have no control, such as genetic inheritance, simply getting older and your ethnic origin – Asians and Afro-Caribbeans do seem to be at a higher risk. Eating lots of sweet things, contrary to popular belief, doesn't cause diabetes, but it leads to weight gain, which does increase your risk. It's a fact that 80% of people with Type 2 diabetes are overweight. The fatter and less fit you are, the greater your risk.

Type 2 diabetes used to be more common in middle age, but increasingly it's affecting younger people too. Those with the condition either don't produce

Here's an idea for you...

How can you get five fruit and vegetables into your daily diet? Try having one piece of fruit at breakfast, plus a piece of fruit after lunch or as an afternoon snack; have a salad with lunch or dinner and two vegetables (not potatoes) with your other meal.

enough insulin or what is produced doesn't work effectively, which means that the body can't use glucose properly and levels remain high in the blood. Some of the symptoms of undiagnosed diabetes include increased thirst, a need to go to the toilet often, especially at night, lethargy and tiredness, blurred vision, regular thrush and genital itching, plus weight loss when nothing else has changed regarding your lifestyle. Doctors say many people have these symptoms on and off for years before eventually being diagnosed as diabetic, which is easily done with a simple blood test.

In the past, if you were diagnosed as having diabetes, physical activity was discouraged and, a high fat/low carbohydrate diet prescribed. How times change! Now exercise is encouraged, just as it is for everyone to improve their health and control weight. As a role model, look to Sir Steve Redgrave, five times Olympic Gold medal winner and a diabetes sufferer! Diet-wise, the reason a high fat diet was recommended was to make up for the lack of calories that resulted from following a low carbohydrate diet to keep sugar levels stable (fat doesn't boost sugar levels in itself). Diabetics are more at risk of heart disease as a result of the condition, but of course, the high fat diet increased this risk! Luckily, nutrition has moved on, with eating guidelines for diabetics pretty much in line with general healthy eating recommendations. As well as using medication and being under strict medical supervision, most diabetics can control their condition and also lose weight by eating in the most healthful way. The eating guidelines also work as a preventative and can be used by everyone. In brief, they are:

- Eat regular meals featuring starchy carbohydrates of the whole grain variety, i.e. wholemeal bread and cereals, rather than refined carbohydrates.

- Cut down on fat, especially saturated fats found in animal products. Choose low fat and monounsaturated fats such as olive oil.

- Eat more fruit and vegetables!

- Cut down on sugar and sugary foods, especially sugary drinks which cause blood glucose levels to rise quickly.

- Cut down on salt to keep blood pressure in check and drink in moderation. Diabetics in particular should be careful of drinking on an empty stomach, as it can precipitate hypoglycaemia – dangerously low blood sugar levels.

'According to one recent study on diabetes care conducted in the US, on average for every 1 kg (2 lb) in weight a person puts on over the normal range, their risk of developing diabetes increases by about 9 per cent.'
JUDITH MILLS, *The Diet Bible*

Defining
idea...

How did it go?

Q   What about special diabetic foods?

A   *Most experts say they are unnecessary and a waste of money.*

Q   Isn't Type 2 diabetes just a mild form of the illness?

A   *No, it needs to be taken seriously. Four out of five people with the condition die prematurely from heart disease. There's also an increased risk of stroke, diabetic vetinopathy which can lead to blindness, and nerve damage in the hands and feet. Action is essential, both if you've already been diagnosed and also as a preventative measure with weight control being an important strategy. Recent research has shown that complications are prevented if blood glucose levels are normalised with Type I diabetes. Most experts believe the same for Type 2 diabetes too.*

Q   Surely it's not that big an issue? What about all the plagues and epidemics?

A   *The World Health Organisation thinks it is a big issue. It is predicting a global epidemic of diabetes, which means that it already is an issue for you and it will definitely be an issue for your children and the ones you might have in the future. Do ask your doctor for a test if any of the risk factors apply to you and also if you have any of the symptoms described above.*

25

Fats: the good, the bad and the downright ugly

Fat friends and foes.

Eating too much of certain fats is definitely harmful to both your waistline and your health, so here are some handy hints on how to perform a bit of liposuction on your diet.

You need to know about fat in food because it's a rich source of calories. In fact, it contains more than twice as many calories, weight for weight, as carbohydrates and proteins.

As well as being a major cause of weight gain, a high-fat diet, particularly one that is high in saturated fats, can also increase your risk of heart disease and breast and bowel cancers.

Fat isn't all bad; our bodies need it. It delivers vitamins A, D, E and K and aids their absorption. It helps to regulate a variety of bodily functions. It makes food taste delicious and gives it a creamy, moreish texture. The thing is not all fats are created equal and we typically consume too much of the wrong kind of fat and not enough

Here's an
idea for
you...

Reach for your extra virgin. A drizzle a day might keep the doctor away. I use olive oil in just about everything. The trouble is that I tend to use lots of it. Yes, it's a healthy oil, but if you eat a lot of it you are just adding unnecessary calories. The key is to measure it. A tablespoon per day is usually enough for everything.

of the good stuff. We should all know our rights from our wrongs for the sake of our health, but there's even more reason to get clued up when there's weight to be lost. So here are the big fat facts to chew on:

■ **Saturated fats** – Foods with high levels of saturated fatty acids include butter, lard, whole milk, hard cheeses, cream, meat and meat products, palm oil and coconut oil. These are the diet wreckers and you should aim to have only a very small amount of them in your daily diet. You can reduce your intake of these kinds of fats by buying leaner cuts of meat and chopping off visible fat. Grilling, baking or steaming foods is a more slimming way to cook than smothering everything in butter and cream.

■ **Trans fats** – These are found in processed foods such as crisps, cakes, biscuits and pies and also in many brands of margarine. Cross the street to avoid them. Check food labels for these fats – they'll be listed as 'hydrogenated'.

■ **Unsaturated fats** – These break down into monounsaturates and polyunsaturates. Monounsaturates are found in olive oil, nut oils, avocados and seeds, which have health benefits for your heart and so are a better choice than saturated fats. But they're still fattening, so use them sparingly. Polyunsaturates pop up in most vegetable oils (corn, sunflower, safflower), fish oils and oily fish. They are generally a good thing, particularly if you consume them in place of saturated fats, although they are still calorific.

'Except for the vine, there is no plant which bears a fruit of as great importance as the olive.'
PLINY

Defining idea...

Overall, fats should make up about a third of your total daily calorie intake, with saturated fats making up less than 10% of all the calories you consume. This rule is just for general health, but as most of us consume too much fat, it should help you lose a couple of kilos. It is quite safe to cut your total intake of all types of fat to about 20% of your daily calories. To reduce the fat you eat, you will probably need to play with the balance of fats in your diet. In the western world, especially in the UK and US, we generally consume a lot of saturated fat. People who live in southern Europe tend to have a better fat balance as they generally eat less dairy, more fish, more plant oils and much more fruit. Think of your favourite region of the Mediterranean and imagine being a local there. How do they eat? French, Italian and Spanish people who live in the countryside tend to eat well-balanced meals prepared from fresh ingredients, avoiding processed foods. If you must drink a lot of milk, try choosing skimmed or half-fat instead of whole milk.

How did it go?

Q If I buy foods marked 'low fat' or 'lite', will I reduce my fat intake?

A *If something is low in fat, it may still be high in calories, so you could still be consuming too many calories to lose weight. Compare the label on a low fat product with the standard version of the product.*

Q How many grams of fat should we eat a day?

A *For average adults of a healthy weight, women should aim for 70 g and men 95 g. When you're trying to lose weight you should be aiming lower. For example, if you are eating around 1800 calories a day, you should go for around 63 g of fat in your diet.*

Q I've read about a slimming pill with a fatty acid in it. Does it work?

A *Conjugated linoleic acid (CLA) is a fatty acid found naturally in many foods, including dairy products and beef. Back in the early 1990s some researchers found that CLA plays a role in keeping body fat levels low and helping lean muscle tissue to develop. Other studies have since found that CLA can improve the body's muscle-to-fat ratio. A pill containing CLA is not a miracle cure, but there does seem to be enough evidence to give it a try. Remember, though, that you will still have to eat less and increase your level of physical activity. Think of CLA as the icing on the cake, not as an excuse to go back to old bad habits!*

26

Ooh, you didn't want to do that...

Unless you have the physique of Manolos, you'd better learn how to lift any weights in a way that protects your back from strain.

East European weightlifters probably practise by playing catch the fridge, but for most of us picking up a heavy bag of shopping or moving an item of furniture is enough to put your back out.

THINK BEFORE YOU LIFT

The bottom line is that if you're not confident that you can lift an object safely because it's too heavy or awkward – don't lift it. Don't take the risk. There's always an alternative way to move it without straining or injuring your back. And if there isn't – well some things are just destined to stay put! The alternatives can even be fun – you could insist on being followed by a moose of a man who does your lifting for you. Or you could take to tottering around on stilettos and refusing to lift a finger except to summon the maitre d'. Admittedly this is harder to pull off if you happen to be male.

Here's an idea for you...

Learn the maximum weight you should lift in a variety of situations. Lifting from below knee height or above shoulder height if close to the body should be limited to 10 (7) kg for men (women); if further away than the length of your forearm, 5 (3.5) kg; at waist height close to the body, 25 (17) kg. Reduce by 10–20% if twisting is involved; if lifting is repeated once or twice per minute, reduce by 20%; and if repeated 12 times per minute, reduce by 80%.

Sometimes it's not a heavy weight that'll do you the damage, but what seems like an easy lift that you do without much thought, especially if your muscles are tired.

There are some situations where you're particularly at risk: twisting at the same time as lifting, or when putting shopping in the back of your car, when you are reaching forwards with a weight in your arms.

At work, it's the incorrect handling of loads that causes many injuries, resulting in pain, time off work and even permanent disablement. Manual handling regulations apply to moving any weights at work, through lifting, lowering, pushing, pulling, carrying, holding or moving, whether these movements are done by hand or using other bodily force. They cover the nature of the force applied. That is the duration, frequency, magnitude and posture you adopt, whether it's an animate load, such as moving people or animals, or inanimate, such as shifting crates. If you think the weights you're being asked to lift at work are too heavy or awkward, then ask your union or manager for an assessment under the manual handling regs. That will startle them!

It may seem to you that you don't do 'lifting' at work anyway. But if your job doesn't normally involve physical effort, you are probably more vulnerable if you're unexpectedly required to lift something such as a water carrier or parcel of photocopier paper than someone who handles heavy weights every day.

HOW SHOULD I LIFT, THEN?

Use a 'straight back/bent knees' posture to hold an object close to your body so that it can fit between your knees while you are lifting it.

That way, the weight you're lifting exerts less leverage on your spine. Get into the habit of bending your knees rather than your back when you go to lift something, hold the object close in towards your body and avoid twisting sideways at the same time as you lift.

When you carry a load you compress your intervertebral discs. This is not usually a problem if the natural curves of the spine are maintained. But if your back is bent forwards or sideways or twisted, an uneven stress is placed on one part of your discs or the ligaments around them, and damage may occur. Loads carried nearer the spine are easier to control, and create less strain on the spine. Twisting, stooping or reaching upwards with a load places more strain on the spine. Loads which are awkward, bulky, prone to shift, or have to be handled in limited spaces or with poor lighting are particular hazards.

Avoid lifting objects that are too heavy. If possible, minimise their weight by splitting them into separate loads. Only lift objects that can be held close to your body. If you can't hold an object close, then use some sort of handling aid. Push rather than pull objects lying on the floor.

'Lifting a barbell ain't like eating no watermelon.'
TOAD, US Olympic weightlifter

Defining idea...

How did it go?

Q **I can't avoid lifting my shopping – my family has the appetite of a pack of professional wrestlers and if I don't keep them fuelled they'll probably eat the furniture. What else can I do?**

A First up, don't overload your shopping bags. Fully laden, they should be no heavier than 3.5 kg (woman) or 5 kg (man). Weigh this out at home so you know what it feels and looks like. Next, make sure there's enough room in your car for you to lift loads in and out without twisting. Consider buying a hatchback if you've not got one already. Finally, why not take your voracious family with you to help with the lifting; you can always leave them in the car if you don't trust them to behave themselves in the supermarket.

Q **Is your 'bent knees/straight back' advice sufficient for someone like me who is a couch potato?**

A No, it probably isn't – but it's a start! Improving your general fitness will help to strengthen your back and keep it flexible, and will thereby help prevent back problems; but it will require a little effort from you, if you feel up to it.

27

Listen to your love muscle

You've been exercising for some time so you're fitter, yes? But how fit? How hard are you working? How do you know if you're in the fat-burning zone or working at your threshold?

Let your heart show you the way.

THE PROBLEM

We all exercise because we're looking for some kind of benefit – lose weight, look better in a T-shirt, drop a clothes size, dodge that heart attack, live longer to enjoy more time with the grandchildren. The problem is that of these admirable goals some are easier to measure than others. When you fit into smaller clothes, weigh what you did when you were in your twenties or see new muscle definition, then you know you got there. But what of those less obvious but often more crucial goals. How do you know when you are fitter? What is fit anyway? Sooner or later as you plug away on a treadmill or stepper, you'll start to wonder if it's really doing any good. And if you can't tell, then what's the point in giving up your precious time when you could be down the pub.

THE SOLUTION

The answer is to listen to your heart, and the way to do that is to invest in a heart rate monitor. There's nothing that complex about heart monitors – at their simplest you have a transmitter on a chest-strap that broadcasts your heartbeats to a small computer/sports watch on your wrist.

Here's an idea for you...

You can do this with even the simplest monitor, or a stopwatch and two fingers as long as (a) you have the patience and (b) you can find an artery with a pulse. Instead of focusing on zones and percentage of maximum, just do your usual session and then see how long it takes your heart rate to drop to 120 (12 beats within a 10 second period if you're doing it manually). As you get fitter that time will drop, and you may find it becomes more accurate to count how long it takes to get down to 100 beats. Not only can you see your cardiovascular fitness improving week by week, but this can also give you early warning of overtraining or infection as a developing cold can whack that recovery time back up by a 10 or 20 second margin.

HOW DOES IT WORK?

Simple though it sounds, having an accurate idea of your heart rate opens a whole new world of accuracy in training. You can now tell exactly how hard you are working, which is often surprisingly different to how hard you think you are working. By seeing how long it takes for your heart to recover from bursts of exercise you now have access to one of the best indicators of how fit you really are.

IN PRACTICE

The first thing with heart rate monitoring is to establish your maximum heart rate. There's a rule of thumb that 220 minus your age gives your maximum. On that basis a forty-year-old would have a maximum heart rate of 180. That's a little imprecise, and there are many other formulae that take account of sex and bodyweight. Because there is this slight variation it's best to follow the instructions that come with your heart monitor.

Once you're at your maximum heart rate, the next step is working out the different training zones. Roughly speaking there are three main training zones: 60–75% of max which is considered easy and often called the 'fat-burning zone', 75–85% of max which is moderate and sometimes referred to as the 'cardio-training zone'; and 85–95% which is giving it some welly and normally only of interest to those going for peak performance and ever-diminishing times.

'My heartbeat is kickin', it's kickin' louder and louder It's getting' deffer and deffer, I'm feelin' prouder and prouder.'
ICE-T, popular vocalist and apparently a man with a keen understanding of the importance of heart rate

Defining idea...

WHAT THE MONITOR DOES, AND HOW TO CHOOSE ONE

The simplest monitors consist of a stop-watch (well you don't want to have two things strapped to your wrist) and will tell you what your rate is. The next step up feature alarms that can be set for zones so, for example, the monitor will beep at you if you get out of the fat-burning zone, or if you drop below a certain level of workload. This is one of the best uses for a monitor and well worth having.

Beyond that level monitors start sprouting all sorts of functions...

- A graphical readout showing a chart of your heartbeat is handy to see how long it takes for your heart to recover after rest.

- A memory of different sessions makes it easy to compare and see your progress.

■ Downloadable details are a delight for the number crunchers who like to plot their progress on a spreadsheet.

■ 'Shielded' transmitters mean you can workout alongside a partner without their monitor interfering with yours.

■ Calorie counters can be programmed with your physical details to monitor how many calories you burn during the day.

■ Programmable sessions mean you can choose an interval session and never look at your watch again – the monitor beeps at you when you have to slow down/speed up and keeps an eye on how hard you're working.

■ GPS is considered the king of the crop right now – the monitor doesn't just watch your heart, it uses satellite tracking to tell you exactly how far you have run/cycled when you're outdoors and what speed you are doing at any moment.

Q **Why would I need a monitor? I know when I'm giving it some.**

A *What the pros called 'perceived effort' is a tricky area because very motivated individuals tend to block out discomfort and non-motivated ones tend to exaggerate it. The same level of work could appear easy to one and hellish to another. At the top end of the scale your body releases chemicals that suppress the pain when you're really giving it welly and so you may have difficulty knowing just how hard it is. Your heart, however, won't skip a beat or lie to you.*

Q **I feel I'm working easily but my heart rate is sky-high. What's going on?**

A *Are you sure you're not overtraining or coming down with an infection? Either can send your heart rate soaring. Try training at 60–70% of your heart rate for half an hour or more (think of all that fat burning) for a week or two and then go back to your normal efforts. If your heart rate is dangerously high or unpredictable, then see your GP.*

Q **The monitor manual keeps referring to my RHR. What's this?**

A *Resting heart rate (RHR) is strictly speaking what level your heart settles down to when you're asleep. Unless you have a partner to help read this off in the night it's usually measured at the moment you wake up. Even so, some people wake up stressed about the day ahead and that can give a slightly high reading. You may get a more accurate level as you wake up covered in newspapers on the sofa this Sunday.*

How did it go?

28

Feeling SAD?

For many people, less daylight equals less happiness. Use these illuminating tips to brighten up and avoid another winter of discontent.

Long, dark days getting you down? Sun shortage can cause sadness ranging from dark moods to a condition called seasonal affective disorder or SAD. Learn how to stop dreading the end of autumn and lighten up.

Everyone seems happier in summer, and many of us feel more gloomy when it gets greyer. But some people get depressed every winter. A diagnosis of SAD can only be made after three or more consecutive winters of symptoms. If you feel depressed in winter, so-so in autumn and full of the joys of spring in, um spring, then you're officially SAD. SAD symptoms are similar to non-seasonal depression but rather than losing weight or waking early, if you've got SAD you're more likely to oversleep and reach for the biscuit jar to satisfy carb cravings. People suffer from SAD throughout the northern and southern hemispheres but it is unsurprisingly rare if you live within 30 degrees of the Equator, as daylight hours are long and exceptionally bright.

Here's an
idea for
you...

Plan a 'summer' holiday in winter. A couple of weeks of long daylight hours to tide you over until spring may be just what the doctor ordered. Why just dream of a white (sandy beach) Christmas?

LIGHT RELIEF

In northern Sweden there are only a few hours of winter daylight and some days with no light at all. Stockholm psychiatrists got a group of depressed patients together. They split them into two groups: one group who felt depressed in winter and a second group whose depression didn't change with the seasons. All patients were given treatment with a light box for ten days. Patients in the first group (whose depression had a seasonal pattern) got a lot better with light box treatment. But those in the second group, who felt low whatever the weather, didn't improve much with light treatment.

Want some of what they had? Light boxes are readily available and in some countries, including Switzerland, they're available on the health service. In other places, you'll have to buy your own. If you plump for a light box, use it daily from when your first symptoms appear. You'll need to sit an arm's length away for between sixty and ninety minutes. Sometimes people think they need to stare straight at it, but you don't have to put your life on hold like that. Let's face it, who's got time? You can read, mark student essays, eat, perfect your macramé, in fact anything you like as long as you're reasonably stationary. Many people feel better after three or four days but that wears off unless it's used every day.' Nuff said.

COULD YOU DO WITH A D?

Scientists have discovered that vitamin D supplements help SAD sufferers. They thought vitamin D deficiency might play a role in SAD. No great surprise as it's been called the sunshine vitamin. Ultraviolet rays from sunlight react on your skin, producing a form of vitamin D. People with SAD who took a vitamin D supplement every day for five days noticed a lift in their winter blues. They took 400 IU of vitamin D. Guess how much a teaspoon of cod liver oil contains? 400 IU.

I've yet to meet anyone who likes the taste of cod liver oil, so if you've wrinkled your nose you're in good company and might like to try prawns, sardines, mackerel or salmon instead – these foods are rich in vitamin D. If you're a vegetarian you'll get small amounts of vitamin D from creamy milk and egg yolks. If you've gone the whole hog (so to speak) and are vegan, you'll need to eat fortified foods – like soy milk, margarine and breakfast cereal – and vitamin D supplements.

And if you're prone to the winter blues, try to make the most out of what sunshine there is. Wrap up warm and enjoy a good walk: your vitamin D levels will thank you for it.

'How heavy the days are. There is not a fire that can warm me, nor a sun to laugh with me.'
HERMAN HESSE, *Steppenwolf*

Defining idea...

How did
it go?

Q **I've heard that taking a single but very high dose of vitamin D is as effective as light therapy. Would it do me any harm?**

A *It's important to remember that although vitamin D is a naturally occurring substance, it can be harmful. It is extremely toxic at high doses, so if you're tempted to crank up your dose, discuss it with your doctor first.*

Q **Is it really necessary to buy a light box. My husband is an artist and uses daylight effect light bulbs. Could I sit by one of those?**

A *Sorry, but these light bulbs just aren't up to the job. Light is measured in lux. The sort of full-spectrum bulbs used by artists which mimic natural light emit around 200–500 lux, whereas the lowest dose you can get away with to treat SAD is 2500 lux. Light boxes emit around 10,000 lux. Might sound high, but not when you realise the light emitted on a sunny day can be up to 100,000 lux. Which is a lot of light bulbs.*

Q **I feel low every year when it starts to get dark earlier and have started using a light box every evening. I'm now having trouble sleeping. Could this be a side effect of light therapy?**

A *Sadly yes. Light boxes can cause side effects. The commonest ones are headaches, sore eyes, feeling squirmy or problems getting to sleep. Try using your light box in the mornings instead and your sleep should improve.*

29

Let them eat greens

If you're struggling to get your child to eat one portion of veg a day – let alone the recommended three – don't despair, there are some relatively simple ways to get him to eat more of the good stuff.

So just what is it about vegetables that makes so many children refuse to eat them?

There are many reasons why your child may be making such a fuss over his greens. But the good news is, there are also lots of ways you can encourage him to change his habits.

A BID FOR INDEPENDENCE

Refusing to eat certain foods, especially those the parent wants him to eat, makes a small child feel independent and grown up. This is very common behaviour between the ages of five and six, but can also be true of older children.

If this sounds like your child, try not to make a big deal of his refusal to eat veg and, instead, look for other ways for him to exercise control in his life. Small children could start choosing what to wear every day; older children could be allowed to decide their bedtime on a weekend night, for example.

Here's an idea for you...

Use root vegetables such as sweet potato, parsnips, uncooked beetroot and swede to make unusual (and slightly sweet) vegetable crisps. Slice the vegetables thinly, toss in a little oil, and lay out – without overlapping – on a baking tray. Bake in a pre-heated oven at 190C/375F/Gas 5 for 20 minutes, then flip your crisps over and bake for a further 10–15 minutes until cooked.

EXPRESSING ANGER

By rejecting food a parent has worked hard to prepare, a small child could be expressing anger or resentment that he cannot put into words.

Perhaps he hasn't had enough attention lately? Maybe you have chastised or punished him for something he feels is just not fair? This type of food rejection is likely to be accompanied by tears and tantrums.

If this sounds like the stand-off in your home, think about what might be the cause of the underlying emotional distress and try to address it.

PLAYING COPYCAT

Younger siblings will often copy their older brothers and sisters. So if your older children are being awkward about eating their veggies – the younger one might start too. Stay relaxed and neutral. Continue to serve vegetables at every meal and ignore any rejection. The fad will quickly pass if it doesn't get a reaction.

To ensure that your child really does end up eating his greens – try the following tips too:

- Don't make compromises. Only buy and serve the foods that you want your child to eat.
- Eat vegetables yourself to set the right example.
- Many children may not like eating cooked vegetables – but will eat them raw. Try carrot batons, baby sweetcorn, fresh peas in pods, celery and sweet red pepper strips.
- Remember veggies don't have to be green. Offer brightly coloured alternatives such as sweetcorn, peppers, sweet potatoes and swede. You can use them to garnish a dish and make it look more exciting.
- Let your child help to plan menus, shop for, and prepare the food.
- Tell him he has to choose two vegetables to go with supper – even if he's not going to eat them himself.
- Try to find a good role model. If you know of a child who eats up their greens, invite them to tea and lavish praise on their eating habits in front of your child.
- Keep the dessert well out of sight until the main course is finished.
- Don't give too much attention to your child when he says he won't eat something. Instead, reinforce the positive by commenting when he does eat the right foods.

And if all the previous advice fails? Resort to stealth tactics. Hide those veggies in casseroles, stews and pasta sauces by puréeing a handful or two of steamed veg and simply stirring it into your child's favourite food.

'I do not like broccoli. And I haven't liked it since I was a little kid and my mother made me eat it. I am President of the United States, and I'm not going to eat any more broccoli.'
GEORGE BUSH SR

Defining idea…

129

How did it go?

Q **My daughter is only interested in chocolate at the moment. There's no way she will eat anything green.**

A *Try making this chocolate courgette cake with her, then. It may not be the healthiest way to encourage her to eat her greens – but hey, it's a start! Line a 20x35cm baking tray with baking paper and preheat the oven to 190°C/350°F/Gas5. Beat together 125g/4 oz softened butter, 125ml/4 fl oz sunflower oil, 1 tsp vanilla extract, 200g/7oz soft brown sugar and 100g/3 oz caster sugar until fluffy. Gradually add three eggs, beating well after each one, and then 125ml/4 fl oz milk until mixed thoroughly. Fold 350g/12oz plain flour, 2 tsp baking powder and 4 tbsps cocoa into the mixture. Stir in 450g/1lb peeled and grated courgettes and pour the mixture into the tin. Bake for 35–45 minutes until cooked through. Leave to cool in the tin.*

Q **My son will only eat potato. It's driving me crazy!**

A *Most children love potatoes in all their guises, so try mixing other puréed vegetables into mashed potatoes – swede works well, as does carrot, sweet potato and parsnips. Pour a tomato and vegetable sauce over a baked spud or roast root vegetable batons in the oven with a little oil to make alternative 'chips'.*

30

Get in the swim

Not been in the pool since you were at school? You're missing out on what could be the perfect anti-ageing exercise.

Swimming is in a league of its own. It's a cardiovascular workout that achieves the incredible feat of targeting every muscle in your body while putting virtually no pressure on your joints.

Exercising in water is like a good relationship – it's completely supportive but it also works you hard enough so that you grow stronger. You may not think so, but swimming is the ideal exercise for anyone who feels self-conscious about their body. OK, the dash from changing room to pool isn't much fun (tip: wear a towel and leave it by the side of the pool) but once you've submerged, it's impossible for anyone to scrutinize the size of your thighs, something you could never say about a multi-mirrored gym. Done in a local pool, swimming is one of the cheapest – and most accessible – ways to exercise, and it doesn't depend on the weather.

Here's an idea for you...

Want to instantly improve your swimming? Buy some goggles. They're vital to help you relax in the water. If you're squinting, your neck muscles are tense and you're much more likely to hold your head out of the water which puts pressure on your back. But don't buy cheap ones – it's a false economy; they'll leave marks on your face and fog up easily so you won't wear them.

Of course, what we're really interested in is how swimming can stave off ageing. The definitive study assessing whether regular swimmers have a biological age that's younger than their calendar age is currently under way, but recent research already suggests that regular endurance exercise such as swimming could make you on average six years younger than a couch potato.

So if it's so great, why don't more of us do it? Basically, because we're not much good at it. Throw the average adult in a swimming pool and they do a contorted breaststroke with their head half out of the water and neck in a spasm, or a frantic front crawl that involves a lot of thrashing, kicking and head turning (and inconvenience for other swimmers). Most of us still swim the way we learned when we were desperately trying not to drown during childhood lessons at the local pool.

The answer? A swimming coach – cheaper than a personal trainer. A swimming coach will iron out the kinks and bad habits in your stroke until you're gliding effortlessly through the water. The newest teaching techniques draw on the body-alignment principles of the Alexander Technique, and the emphasis is on helping you reach a state of deep relaxation in the water. And, because your muscles are in perfect alignment, after thirty minutes of effortless powering through the pool, you will feel like you've had a massage. Done properly, swimming becomes a kind of moving meditation that you can keep up for hours.

'For each hour you exercise, you get roughly two extra hours of life.'
DR RALPH PAFFENBARGER, epidemiologist

Defining idea...

Taking lessons is also the best way to get yourself out of a one-stroke rut. Most people find one stroke suits them best and it can be tempting just to plough up and down doing it, even if it does give you a stiff neck or tired shoulders. But alternating your strokes means you will work harder, burn off more calories and target more muscles. A coach can also design workout programmes specifically for you, using different speeds and strokes as well as equipment like floats, to get maximum results. What are you waiting for? Dive in!

How did
it go?

Q   **I know how you breathe is important when you're swimming. But how do I know if I'm doing it right?**

A   *Most people take a huge deep breath in, then hold it when their face is under water. It's part of the anxiety many of us have about being in water – even the strong and experienced swimmers among us. To feel relaxed in the water, you should breathe normally, and never hold your breath. Try breathing out gently through the mouth when your face is in the water, then when your head comes back up, you're ready to take another breath.*

Q   **Is there anything to do in the pool except endless lengths?**

A   *How about aqua-jogging? It's as good at improving the cardiovascular system as jogging on land, and without the injury potential. It also burns around twelve calories a minute, compared with six calories a minute for breaststroke, so you can halve your time spent in the pool and burn off as much fat. All you need is an aqua-buoyancy jogging vest or belt (some pools will lend you one, or look on fitness equipment websites), and a pool deep enough so your feet don't touch the bottom. (Oh, and a certain amount of imperviousness to being stared at – at least at first.) Use the same arm movements as you would running on land. Flex and point your feet as you stride, as this will help your stability in the water. It also strengthens the muscles of the front and back of the legs. Warm up for three minutes by walking the shallow end of the pool four times. Roll your shoulders and stretch your arms above your head. Move to the deep end and do nine minutes of aqua-jogging. End with a three-minute cool down by walking in the shallow end again.*

31

Water babies

Seventy per cent of the planet is covered in water, and when we're born 70% of us is water too. It's cool to be wet, so why aren't you drinking enough of the stuff?

There are life forms that can live without oxygen, but none last long without water. So why do we pay so little attention to it?

Do you know what constantly amazes me? People who go to a posh restaurant, spend a fortune on the meal and then think they're being clever by asking for a glass of tap water. Granted, some places seem to charge more for water than for wine, but is this a smart way of saving money? Most tap water tastes disgusting. I realise that this is my personal opinion, so do your own survey. The most unpalatable glass I ever had was in England's rural Oxfordshire. It was like drinking part of a swimming pool. Even London water tastes better despite, so legend has it, having passed through eight other bodies first. However, is changing to bottled water the solution?

BOTTLED BLISS?

Bottled water isn't always the purest water. In fact, it might actually contain more bacteria than the tap version. Most tap water, however, will contain a cocktail of

Here's an idea for you...

If you find 2-litre bottles of water too intimidating, try the small ½-litre bottles instead. If you're not used to drinking masses of water, increase your intake slowly by just one ½-litre bottle a day at first. If it feels like trying to rehydrate hard-baked earth after a drought, add some lecithin into your diet as this will help make your cells more permeable to water.

contaminates, most commonly lead, aluminium and pesticides. Also, the labelling on bottled water makes it far from clear in terms of what you're getting.

Generally, water can be called natural mineral water, spring water or table water. Mineral water is generally from a pure, underground source, where the rocks and earth have naturally filtered it. Spring water also comes from a filtered underground source, but does not have to be bottled on the spot. Table water is definitely the dodgiest dude of all as it's the least defined and could be a mix of water including tap water so unless you really like the design of the bottle you could just be wasting your money. Watch out for artificially carbonated table and spring water as this can rob the vital minerals in the body by binding to them. Also, look at the proportion of minerals – remember that salt (sodium) will dehydrate the body slightly.

Every now and then, there'll be a TV programme featuring blokes turning into women or male fish turning into female fish. Scare stories aside, the point is that we're being continuously exposed to xeno-oestrogens (foreign oestrogens) in our environment and these can have a feminising effect on our bodies. One source of these foreign oestrogens is through plastics – the worst thing you can do is leave your water heating up in the sun in a plastic bottle. So, blokes shouldn't simply blame their boobs on beer (although alcohol also has feminising effects, but that's another story!).

'Water, water, everywhere,
Nor any drop to drink.'
SAMUEL TAYLOR COLERIDGE, *The Rime of the Ancient Mariner*

Defining idea...

WATER WORKS

What are the best choices then? Well, one cheap solution is to get a filter jug, which removes the bug-busting chlorine element. The carbon filter also takes out some minerals, so another top tip is to change the filter at regular intervals to prevent manky old ones from leaching bacteria back into your drinking water. The jug should be kept in your fridge.

Another option would be to have a filter attached to your tap so that water is continuously filtered or you might want to consider the more expensive, but definitely superior, reverse osmosis systems which separate the water from the other elements that are contained in it. This is what NASA developed for its astronauts (you don't want to think about why they're filtering water!).

How did
it go? **Q I drink plenty of tea and coffee so surely I must be getting enough liquid to rehydrate me?**

A *Unfortunately, this isn't going to do it as both tea and coffee are dehydrating. The diuretic effect of these beverages means that they rob the body of more than they supply. I know it's a challenge, but cut down on the amount of tea and coffee you drink. Like everything else, it's just a habit. At first, it will be a struggle but once your body realises how thirsty it is, you'll find that you'll be naturally reaching out for water rather than the colas. The phase where you need to pee more will also pass (excuse the pun), as your body will absorb the water rather than it going right through you. And since it goes through you surprisingly quickly, sipping water rather than glugging huge glasses of the stuff will help. By the way, you'll also begin to like water, rather than expecting what you drink to have flavour!*

Q What about oral rehydration therapy and isotonic drinks?

A *Save the oral rehydration therapy (a mixture of salts and sugar) for when you've got cholera – though some people swear by it as a hangover cure! Isotonic drinks are really intended to help athletes absorb water and energy quickly. Some are loaded with sugar – you've been warned!*

32

PMS busters

Ten top tips to beat the monthly blues.

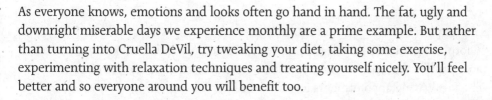

One thing guaranteed to scupper any get-gorgeous plan is PMS. Loathed by women and feared by men, PMS has become synonymous with big pants, the biscuit tin and a really, really bad mood.

As everyone knows, emotions and looks often go hand in hand. The fat, ugly and downright miserable days we experience monthly are a prime example. But rather than turning into Cruella DeVil, try tweaking your diet, taking some exercise, experimenting with relaxation techniques and treating yourself nicely. You'll feel better and so everyone around you will benefit too.

EXERCISE

The 'time of the month' excuse may well have got you out of PE, but exercise is actually a great PMS buster. In the days just before your period, there's an increase in oestrogen, which can cause fluid retention and make you bloated and lethargic. Exercise boosts circulation and helps release this excess fluid. Also, increasing blood

Here's an idea for you...

Add a drop or two of geranium oil to a nice warm bath and have a long soak. According to aromatherapists it has balancing effects on our hormones.

circulation in your abs can help alleviate cramps, so ease period pains by doing some crunches or sit-ups.

LOOK AFTER YOUR SKIN

Premenstrual hormone changes can influence sebum production, which may make your skin oilier and more prone to spots. Some women find taking the Pill can help control breakouts. Otherwise, get yourself an effective over-the-counter treatment or try tea tree oil, a great natural antibacterial. Keep your skin meticulously clean and cover spots with a dab of concealer the same shade as your skin or with a dab of foundation from the dry part of the lid.

BE KIND TO YOURSELF

Some experts believe that your monthly hormone changes affect your body's endorphins (natural painkillers). That's why treatments such as waxing may be more painful, and why you may feel anxious, depressed or suffer from insomnia. Schedule waxing appointments for earlier or later in the month when you're feeling more resilient and instead boost your mood with a gentle massage, pedicure or fabulous blow-dry.

CHANGE YOUR DIET

Omega-3 fats regulate hormone function and have been found to help alleviate PMS symptoms. So, eat fish such as salmon, trout, mackerel and herring.

Cutting down on wheat can help alleviate bloating. In stir-fries and salads swap meat for soya-based foods like tofu, as they're full of isoflavones, which can help regulate hormonal imbalances. Tofu is also a good source of magnesium and calcium, which have anti-inflammatory effects.

Studies have shown a deficiency of magnesium can cause or exacerbate symptoms of PMS and that eating magnesium-rich foods can help ease water retention, headaches, mood swings, fatigue and period cramps. Best sources include green leafy vegetables, nuts and pulses; eat them with protein foods such as meat, chicken and fish, and with regular intakes of calcium-rich foods to help its absorption.

GO EASY ON THE BOOZE

Alcohol seems to be absorbed more rapidly into the bloodstream just before your period and takes longer to metabolise, so you may get drunk more easily. Drink plenty of water – one glass for each glass of alcohol – and make sure you eat with your booze. Swap nasty plonk for just one delectable glass of expensive fizz and you'll avoid that hangover head (and face).

DRINK TONS OF WATER

Water can help alleviate that horrid fluid retention. Cut down on salt too, as the more salt you consume, the more your body holds on to water to avoid dehydration. Flavour your food with parsley or lemon juice instead. And try swapping caffeine for herbal teas.

Defining idea...

'Women complain about premenstrual syndrome, but I think of it as the only time of the month that I can be myself.'
ROSEANNE BARR

TRY SUPPLEMENTS

There's good evidence that calcium supplements taken with magnesium can help relieve premenstrual cramps. They may also improve problems of water retention. Vitamin B6 supplements can also help. It's thought to lift low moods because it helps to raise levels of the mood-enhancing chemical serotonin.

GET SOME FOOT THERAPY

Reflexology may be effective, too. Studies show that women who had ear, hand and foot reflexology for two months had a significant reduction in PMS symptoms. They said they felt better two months after finishing the therapy too, so it may have long-lasting benefits.

DE-STRESS

Tiredness and stress can trigger PMS symptoms or make them worse. Treat yourself to a massage or a pampering spa day. Or spend a cosy evening in; turn off the phone, light some scented candles and cuddle up in front of a video with a face pack on.

GET EARLY NIGHTS

Your beauty sleep may suffer just before your period due to a drop in the hormones that help promote slumber. Aim to get to bed earlier and to help you drop off try drinking camomile tea or milk with a teaspoon of honey, or put lavender on your pillow. Natural remedies passionflower or valerian may also help.

Q   I get really bad backache during my period. Are there any exercises that might help?

A   Try the yoga move known as the Child's Pose. Kneel on the floor, separating your knees slightly, and sit back on your heels. Put a rolled-up towel across the tops of your thighs, then lean forward and rest your forehead on the floor. Relax your arms alongside your body, with your palms face up. Hold for at least thirty seconds, breathing deeply.

Q   Why do I crave chocolate just before my period?

A   Women with PMS have lower levels of serotonin (known as 'nature's Prozac'), a chemical produced in your body that makes you feel good. You may therefore crave sweet foods as a way of replacing this. Another theory is that you're more likely to experience low blood sugar levels because of fluctuating hormones, so grab sugary snacks as quick energy sources. The best advice is to eat little and often, eat plenty of protein to fill you up, and choose healthy snacks such as fruit, crackers and yoghurt. If you must indulge, pick high-quality chocolate or organic ice cream.

Q   How can I ease breast pain?

A   Try evening primrose oil, which has been found to make your breasts less sensitive to hormonal changes. Lowering your intake of saturated fat, which is found in pies, meat and pastries, may also help.

How did it go?

33

A handful of dirt

Dirt never did anyone any harm (live burial notwithstanding), and in fact can be good for you. You wouldn't think that the garden is the best place for you and your allergy, but it may be just what you need.

Permission to get dirty, sir? Permission granted. But we're not talking special phone numbers or websites here, we're talking about common or garden everyday dirt.

It's a fact of life that when children play they get messy. That puddle is to jump in, some food should go on my face and onto the floor, this wet mud makes rather cost-effective Play-Doh, don't you think mum? It's how they learn. Adults, on the other hand, like things clean, well most people do. In fact, the increasing number of personal, household and even garden hygiene products now available confirms that we have become cleanliness obsessed. Just look at the hermetically sealed boxes the style gurus are promoting in home-style magazines. Nah. It doesn't work. The pristine white sofa may look fabulous 'dahling', but to keep it this way you certainly don't sit on it, lie on it, or do whatever else you do on a sofa. Well, not after you've taken the plastic cover off it. It's crazy, isn't it? I have actually seen a table lamp in someone's home with the plastic still on the shade, and it was all I could do to

Here's an idea for you... When you need to clean something up off the floor or to clean a household surface, don't go overboard. Just use a damp cloth and keep the household cleaning products for the special things in life. There's no need to have a sterile environment, which is impossible to achieve anyway. With this idea you'll save yourself time, energy, and some money too.

prevent myself from ripping it off. It's almost as bad as taking perfectly good household items such as lamps and picture frames and covering them in seashells. Though no one would really do that, would they?

At the moment the adults are winning, and cleanliness, if not next to godliness, is at least next door in the dining room. But if we want to win the war on allergies, we may just have to spend a little less time spraying, wiping and washing everything in sight.

For some time now experts in the field of allergy have come to believe that something called the 'hygiene hypothesis' may help to explain the meteoric rise in the number of people with allergies. It goes something like this. If our immune system is exposed to harmless bacteria and viruses early in life, one type of cell in our immune system, the Th1 cells, takes control and trains the body to recognise which foreign invaders pose a threat and which don't. The immune system thus develops normally. If, however, our immune system is not presented with this opportunity to learn, then other immune cells, the Th2 cells, are stimulated. This is bad news, as they try to take control and allergy develops.

Siblings, day care, farms and animals are all good for us, since these may provide the exposure to harmless bugs needed to reduce the risk of allergy developing. Research has found that children who wash their hands more than five times a day and who have two baths a day are more likely to get asthma than those who wash and bath less frequently than this. Other research has identified that teenagers who grew up on farms and were exposed to animals were much less likely to develop asthma than those who did not. Also, children with older brothers or sisters are less likely to develop allergies than only children or first-borns. Now this may not be the whole story, but research like this suggests that being a little grubby is no bad thing.

'In order for something to become clean, something else must become dirty.'
IMBESI's Conservation of Filth Law

Defining idea…

Not long ago I saw a television advert for a household cleaner which proclaimed how certain items of furniture, for example tabletops, can be heavily laden with bacteria, even more than the toilet itself. Shock horror! It implied that allowing your child or baby to be exposed to these was tantamount to abuse. But most of these bacteria are harmless, and coming into contact with them is unlikely to cause your child harm; on the contrary, it may do her some good by helping to train her immune system to learn that these bacteria are OK, they're harmless. The bottom line is that the hygiene hypothesis says we have become too clean, and in doing this we have allowed allergy to take over.

How did it go?

Q   So I don't need to wash then?

A   *Sure, if you want friends to stop calling and people to move away from you on the bus. The theory behind the hygiene hypothesis is not that we shouldn't wash, but that we shouldn't overdo it. There's no need for a sterile environment. Anyway, if you remove harmless bacteria, you provide an opportunity for the dangerous stuff to move in.*

Q   But it's not all down to hygiene, is it?

A   *It's true that the hygiene hypothesis is only one part of the answer, an answer that is still far from complete. In fact, it's only a theory and not a proven fact. Genetics, environment, development and how much allergen a person is exposed to probably all play their part too. Development of allergies is not a simple process and we are still some way from fully understanding it.*

Q   At what stage in life can this hygiene thing have any influence?

A   *It's believed that the battle for control between the Th1 and Th2 cells isn't settled until children are in their first years at school. In fact, this battle may continue right through to adolescence, when another inter-body battle starts – the battle of the puberty hormones. So, based on this, there is still a chance of influencing the process of whether allergy occurs right up until the teenage years. By adulthood it's probably too late, but who knows, in future we may find that even as late on as this there may still be a chance of influencing the development of allergies.*

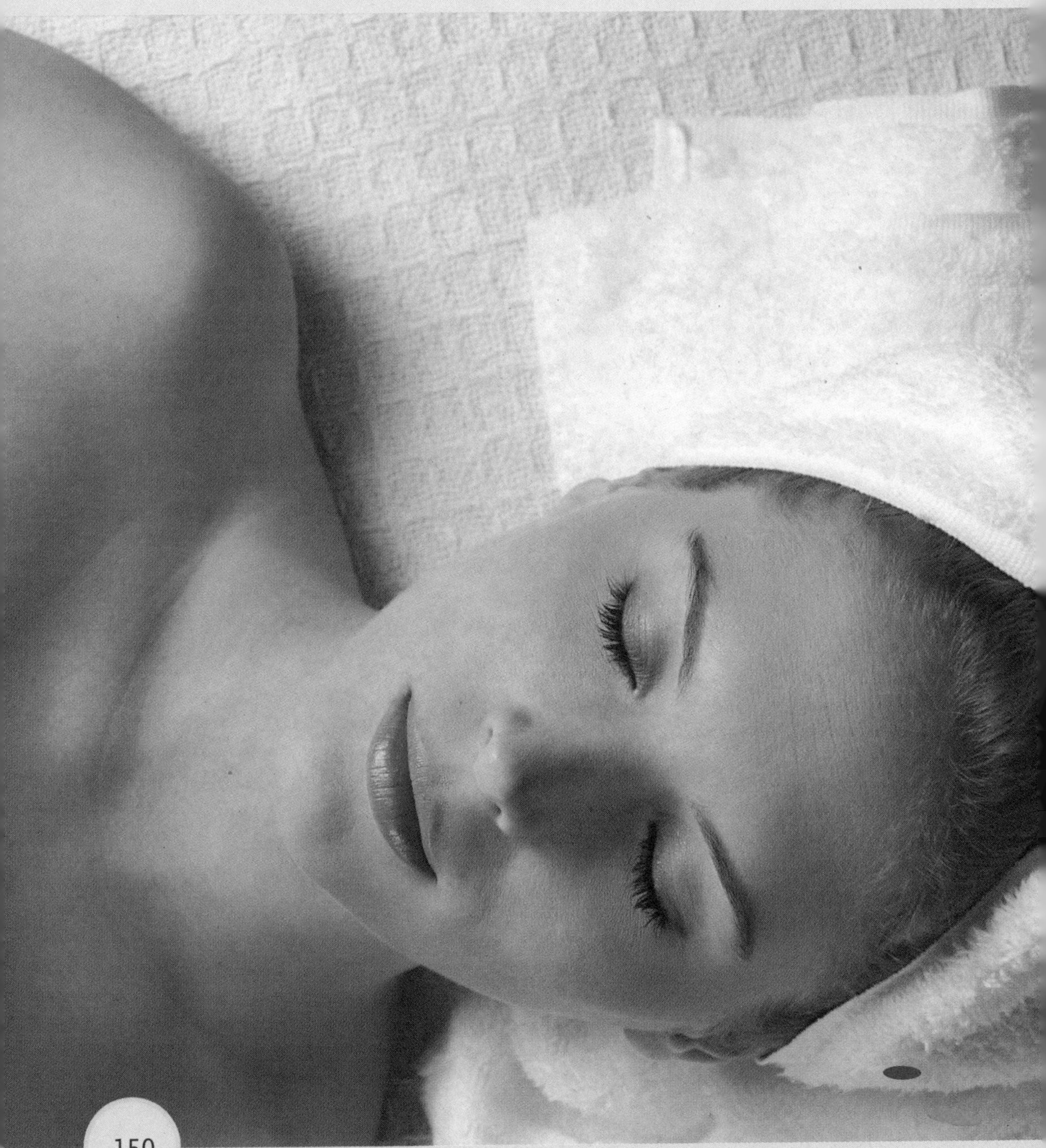

34

Restoration day

When you're suffering from chronic, long-term stress. When your batteries are blown. When burnout is imminent, here is your emergency plan.

Book yourself a day out. By tomorrow, you will feel rested, stronger and more in control. (No, don't stop reading — you can make this happen.)

All you need is twenty-four hours. If you have children, ask someone else to look after them for as much of the day as possible. Remember that if you don't look after yourself, you will have nothing left to give to others.

The restoration day is based on three principles:

- Replenishing your body by giving it rest.

- Resting your brain by focusing on your body.

- Nourishing your soul with healthy simple food which will replenish the nutrients stripped away by stress.

Here's an idea for you...

Go to bed at 9.30 p.m. today and every day this week if you can manage it. Don't watch TV if you're not tired – read or listen to music. People who do this have turned around their stress levels in a week.

Before you get up

When you wake, acknowledge that this day will be different. Today you are going to shift the emphasis onto relaxation and releasing tension and replacing what stress has drained away from your body. Stretch. If you feel like it, turn over and go back to sleep. If not, read an inspirational tome – a self-help book, poetry, a favourite novel. Don't reach for your usual coffee or tea. Sip a mug of hot water with lemon: this, according to naturopaths, boosts the liver which has to work incredibly hard processing all the junk that goes into your body. Whatever, it's soothing. Every time panic hits because you're not doing anything – now and for the rest of the day – breathe in deeply for a count of eight and out for a count of eight.

When you get up

Stretch for ten minutes. A few yoga stretches are good, but it doesn't matter as long as you try to stretch every muscle in your body. You don't have to do this 'perfectly', it's not a workout, it's a reminder – you have a body: it carries tension and pain. Feel the cricks draining out. Finish with the yoga position known as the Child's Pose. Kneel with your legs tucked under you. Bend forward so your forehead rests as near to the floor as possible in front of you. A cushion on your knees might make this more comfortable. Take your arms behind you with hands pointing back and palms upward. Rest like this and breathe deeply. This is a favourite of mine because it releases tension in the neck and shoulders, which is where I store tension. I've been known to climb under my desk at work and do this for a few moments.

Breakfast

Try a fruit smoothie: blend a cup of natural yogurt with one banana and a couple of handfuls of other fruits; peach, mango, strawberries, pineapple. Thin, if preferred, with a little fruit juice. Sip slowly, preferably outside. Imagine the vitamin C zooming around your body replacing the levels depleted by stress. My advice today is to eat lightly and avoid (except for the odd treat) foods that strain digestion too much. Drink coffee and tea if you normally do; the last thing you want is a caffeine withdrawal headache. But don't have more than, say, three caffeine drinks. Caffeine will make you jittery even if you're very used to it.

'Rest as soon as there is pain.'
HIPPOCRATES

Defining idea...

Morning

Get outside – in the most natural surroundings you can manage. Ideally, lie on your back on the grass. Stare at the sky. Let your mind drift off. Or walk in the countryside, the park, sit in your garden. If you really can't bear to be still, do some gardening.

Lunch

Have a huge salad combining every colour of vegetable you can think of – green, yellow, orange, purple, red. More vitamin C. Serve with a delicious dressing. This meal must include one absolute treat – a glass of wine, a dish of ice-cream, a piece of chocolate. Lie back. Indulge.

Afternoon

Go back to bed, or curl up on a cosy corner of your sofa. Watch a favourite movie, or a comedy show. A weepie can be great for this. A good cry is very therapeutic. Sleep if you can. Or if you'd prefer, listen to some favourite music.

Dinner

You should be hungry but feeling light. Eat another pile of vegetables – a salad or perhaps a stir-fry, following the 'eat a rainbow' advice given above. Have a fresh piece of fish grilled or fried in a little oil or butter. Think delicious but simple. Present your food beautifully; eat it by candlelight.

Go to bed early. Resist the temptation to watch TV. Read a book, listen to the radio or some music.

How did it go?

Q   Can't I just stay in bed?

A   *Better than nothing but it won't relax you as much as following a structured programme. The restoration day looks deceptively simple but it works on a deeper level. I've lain in bed all day when I've been stressed and I've done this – this works much much better.*

Q   What about exercising?

A   *Formalise the stretches by going to a yoga class if you really must, but although exercising is terrific for stress, it's not part of the restoration day because it brings a competitive everyday vibe. Today should feel like a holiday from your usual programme – a change really is as good as a rest. I suggest taking a day off work rather than doing this at the weekend. Knowing everyone else is working doubles the efficacy!*

35

Loads of alternatives

Do you use complementary medicine? Once people might have thought you were weird, but these days so many of us use complementary medicines, you'd be weird not to give one a try.

Many complementary and alternative medicines are based on the opinion that they probably work, rather than lots of evidence that they actually cure people. But there's little evidence that they don't work, either.

Some complementary practitioners are also doctors, physiotherapists or nurses who are state registered with their own professional bodies. Others, such as osteopaths and chiropractors, are registered with their own statutory bodies; in France and Germany, it's mostly medically trained doctors who practise complementary therapy. Most complementary practitioners have completed some form of further education in their discipline. But their knowledge and skills mainly come from training based on what has been passed down by tradition rather than actually proven by hard scientific evidence. That's no reason to write them off, however.

Here's an idea for you...

Many of the alternative therapies involve other people touching you with their hands. The exclusive attention of a therapist in treating you for fifteen minutes or more can make you feel good and cared for; you'll leave an alternative therapy session feeling marvellous after this kind of treatment. With conventional health care, a prescription for a drug promises benefits sometime in the future, not right now, in the present. Maybe you could pick and mix complementary therapies and conventional health care with the same practitioner – they can coexist and you'll be the winner. Don't go to more than one practitioner at a time, though; their treatments might conflict and they won't necessarily know what each other is doing.

There are physical, psychological, social and spiritual problems connected to all human illness. Your body has the capacity for self-repair. A complementary practitioner treats each person as an individual. Their holistic package of care for you will include advice about your lifestyle, counselling, relaxation, diet and exercise as well as their particular therapy for your troubles and symptoms.

There are some common features between the various kinds of complementary therapies. Some of the terms used such as 'oi/chi' or 'prana energy' have no equivalent in western medical culture. Such energy is thought to travel through channels – chakras or meridians – as in acupuncture. Diseases of specific organs or systems of the body are linked to particular mental or emotional patterns of symptoms; for example, anxiety and fear might cause digestive disturbances: you'll know that from when you get a dodgy stomach on the morning of an exam or before an important interview. Holistic treatments try to clear and balance these disturbed energies by working on your body's self-healing capacity and provoking a positive immune response rather than targeting specific symptoms or diseases. Many doctors and nurses practise in this holistic manner too. Holistic practitioners believe that your illness provides you with an opportunity for making positive changes as you create a better balance to your life.

> **'Let's be clear about the boundaries. A broken leg requires hospitalisation, full stop. A diseased appendix needs to be removed, full stop. But recovery from appendicitis is likely to be aided by complementary care and a strong immune system.'**
> PETER HAIN, UK politician

Defining idea...

Some people try complementary medicine because they're desperate, when they've tried all the conventional treatments without success. Others like alternative medicines because they seem low-tech compared to conventional healthcare, or may be sceptical about the benefits or dangers of conventional treatments prescribed by doctors. The feeling of being in control of the various treatments – because you pay for complementary therapies – appeals to some people. There are so many different approaches that you should find something to help you: so long as you can afford it.

On the whole, we don't know how many of the alternative therapies are effective for exactly which conditions; for example, just because acupuncture is effective for lower back pain, doesn't necessarily mean that it's also effective for controlling or preventing chest pain or angina. Most people don't care why a certain remedy works, just that it does. And for some it might be the placebo effect – the fact that they're taking a treatment – that makes them think it's working. If someone listens to you with interest and uses their hands to massage or treat you, you're likely to leave them feeling better. And the jury is still out in many areas: lots of people advocate various vitamins for preventing heart disease, for instance, while others report that multivitamins cannot stop people with heart problems having further heart attacks or strokes.

How did it go?

Q **I'm confused, as there are so many alternatives to choose from with lots of pros and cons. How can I be sure what treatment I'm getting and what it will do?**

A *Be ready with a checklist of questions and go through them with the therapist when you're considering trying any new treatment. These are the sort of things you could ask: What will this treatment do? How long will I need to be treated for? How much will it cost? Can I take this treatment alongside other treatments or medicines I'm taking? What are my chances of side effects or after effects? This should help clear up your confusion.*

Q **Complementary treatments sound safer than conventional medicines. Are they?**

A *Well, not enough is known about which complementary and alternative medicines do more good than harm. Some forms are safe, but others aren't, so be cautious and do some research yourself. Be careful that you don't get side effects from a clash between therapies, such as a medication prescribed by a doctor and herbal medicine bought over the counter. Always tell your doctor or pharmacist what complementary treatments you're taking, or check carefully on the packet of any complementary therapies you're buying if you're already on prescribed drugs.*

36

Avoiding the revenge of Bacchus

Hangovers are the scourge of every enthusiastic drinker. But because there's no such thing as a hangover cure the most sensible approach is avoidance.

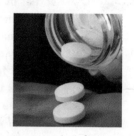

There are treatments that will make you feel slightly less grim than you did before taking them — or will replace one disgusting taste in your mouth with another.

But so far no one has come up with anything that will make you feel as good as you would after an alcohol-free evening and plenty of sleep. The whole point of a hangover is that it's a punishment. As a child you learned that if you ate too much you'd be sick or that if you put your hand near fire you'd get burnt. In the same way, those who drink too much are rewarded with a throbbing head, sluggish metabolism and a mouth that feels like the bottom of a hamster's cage. Their bodies are saying, 'Don't do it again!'

For the free-thinking drinker, wine is not about intoxication – it's about appreciating subtle flavours and aromas. Nevertheless, a gastronomic blow-out that involves matching diverse foods to diverse wines is likely to play havoc with your system.

Here's an idea for you...

Many wine buffs keep a few bottles of wine open at the same time – partly so that they can compare them and also so that they can try them out with different foods. On a day-to-day basis this habit can encourage you to simply taste a couple of wines rather than open a bottle and finish it within a day or two.

THE FREE-THINKING DRINKER'S GUIDE TO HANGOVER AVOIDANCE

If you're taking part in a gastronomic session that involves matching different wines with different courses, make sure that you don't drink more than half a glass of each (wine buffs prefer half-filled glasses anyway because they provide a greater distance between the surface of the wine and your nose, allowing aromas to circulate). Remember, too, that to enjoy a wine you don't need to drink a huge quantity of it – just enough to savour.

Plenty of water is essential – partly because it acts as a brake on the amount of wine that you can drink and partly because it counters the diuretic effect of alcohol. Try to drink a couple of large glasses of water before you get anywhere near an aperitif. This avoids the peril of using wine to quench your thirst. For this purpose, still water is ideal. Fizzy water can bloat you and discourage you from drinking enough of it. Your goal should be to drink at least a large glass of water for every small glass of wine you drink; this is also a good way of cleansing your palate.

The better the wines you drink, the less likely you are to feel the consequences the morning after (there's no clinical evidence for this, just the testaments of millions of well-seasoned drinkers). The other advantage of good-quality wine is that it tends to be more satisfying, so you aren't tempted to drink more than you need.

KNOWING WHEN TO STOP

'My view is that the golden rule in life is never to have too much of anything.'
TERENCE

Defining idea...

The mark of a serial binger is someone who can't make that Pavlovian connection between excessive drinking and the physical pain experienced the morning after. Just remember that your memory of a good meal will be enhanced if it isn't clouded by hazy recollections of its later stages the morning after. Much of the damage is done in the last throes of a meal. Try to avoid the following:

- **Coffee.** Alcohol does enough to disrupt your sleep patterns. Why make them even worse?
- **More than one glass of Port.** Either drink Port when you are sober or drink it sparingly if you are mildly drunk. It might slip down easily but it has an alcohol content of 19%.
- **Spirits.** Is the end of a meal really the time to enjoy your prized single malt? If anything, it should be deployed as an early evening aperitif when you aren't planning to do much drinking.

A NOTE ON HABITUAL DRINKING

Much more dangerous than the occasional binge is developing a pattern of habitual drinking. Even those who consider themselves moderate drinkers find it hard to pass an evening without drinking at least one or two glasses of wine – a number that can all too easily increase to three or four. From this seemingly manageable intake it is easy to slip into a bottle a day habit – particularly at times of stress. The only way to avoid this happening is to ensure that wine consumption doesn't become a habit. Whenever possible try to avoid drinking for two days in succession and make sure that when you drink it is in company rather than alone. Often, when you feel that you need a glass of wine in the early evening it isn't alcohol that you're yearning for but water – try to drink a couple of large glasses of water and see whether the urge passes.

How did it go?

Q   Are there really no effective hangover cures?

A   *At best they are palliative. Rather than putting money and effort into trying to cure a hangover, it's better to avoid getting one in the first place.*

Q   Aren't coffee and digestifs a good way to settle the stomach?

A   *That's one way of looking at it. Remember that the traditional ingredients of the gastronomic blowouts, from aperitifs and ameuse geules to coffee and petit fours, were created for people who didn't have to get up for work the next day.*

37

Saving your senses

The future's bright, so here's what you need to do today to make sure you can see – and hear – it for longer!

Does reading the newspaper these days hurt your arms — because you have to hold it at arms' length to read it? Do you only like reading where there's a bright light available?

This is regarded as part of the eyes' normal ageing process and is known as presbyopia. Normal, healthy, young eyes have a wide range of focus from the far distance to a few centimetres. In a young eye, the lens is very flexible. As we get older, the lens of the eye thickens and slowly loses its flexibility leading to a gradual decline in our ability to focus on objects that are close up. It's why many of us need reading glasses from the age of forty onwards.

But there's also a theory that the loss of focusing ability in later life is mainly due to acquired habits of strain which can be both prevented and reversed. According to American ophthalmologist Dr William Bates, some simple exercises can help. The theory is that vision problems aren't static and can be improved by keeping the eye muscles relaxed and moving freely. Exercises include spending time with your palms over your eyes every day, and choosing a different colour on each day of the

Here's an idea for you...

If you're having trouble hearing, get your ears syringed! Hearing is often dulled by ears full of wax. You can get drops over the counter from a pharmacy to soften the wax. Use it for a week then book an appointment with the nurse at your doctor's surgery to have your ears syringed. You may well be amazed at just how much better you can hear afterwards.

week and consciously looking out for that colour all day. For more information on the Bates method, see www.seeing.org.

But there are more serious eye conditions to avoid as you age. Age-related macular degeneration (or AMD for short) and cataracts are the leading causes of blindness in the developed world. AMD affects 20% of people over the age of sixty-five and cataracts almost 50% of those over seventy-five. But both could be avoided by simply eating more vegetables.

Many people grew up with their mothers saying 'Eat up your carrots, they'll help you see in the dark.' It's just one of the many old wives' tales that have finally been proved true by scientific research. It makes you wonder where those old wives got such accurate insight before laboratories, white coats and doctors were even invented! But that's another story. We now know that the beta-carotene contained in carrots can convert into vitamin A, which has a critical role to play in night vision. We also know that your mother should have added, 'and while you're at it, finish off your dark green vegetables, pumpkin and red peppers'!

These vegetables are all high in a micronutrient called lutein, which helps to stave off the free radical damage thought to cause AMD. Boosting your intake of disease-fighting carotenoids in dark green and orange-yellow vegetables such as carrots, spinach, broccoli and squash will also help. Foods rich in carotenoids (especially spinach, kale and broccoli) will also help you fend off cataracts, as will vitamins C (from fruits and veg) and E (found in vegetable oils, nuts and seeds, egg yolks and green leafy vegetables). If you're a fan of the 'belt-and-braces' approach, up your vegetable intake, and take a daily multivitamin supplement. It could reduce your long-term cataract risk by 60%, according to one study.

'Keep your eyes on the stars, and your feet on the ground.'
THEODORE ROOSEVELT

Defining idea...

Hearing is also a vital sense for keeping us in touch with the world around us. Many people find their hearing becoming less acute once they are past the age of fifty, and a majority of those over seventy have some degree of hearing loss. This happens as the cochlea in the inner ear become less effective at picking up sound, especially high-pitched ones. Most experts now agree that people could avoid long-term hearing loss by simply avoiding loud noises. If you refuse to give up those heavy metal concerts, at least wear earplugs. And never be tempted to leave off your protective ear muffs if you work in a noisy environment.

Your hearing will not normally be tested at a routine check-up but if you suspect it has deteriorated, your doctor may do some preliminary tests or refer you for specialist investigation.

'Of all the senses, sight must be the most delightful.'
HELEN KELLER, who was both blind and deaf

Defining idea...

How did it go?

Q I can't really follow a conversation in a noisy environment any more but I really don't want to wear a hearing aid. What else can I do?

A *Unfortunately there is no cure for the age-related decline in hearing but hearing aids can make a world of difference. Are memories of an ancient uncle whose hearing aid used to whistle away putting you off? Technology has moved on massively and today's devices are silent, and so tiny they're undetectable. Of course, avoiding places with lots of background noise such as bars and restaurants can help. But if you're also finding it difficult to follow a conversation in any social environment, see your doctor for a referral to a hearing specialist. Cutting yourself off from socialising is one of the fastest ways to speed up the ageing process.*

Q I don't want to wear reading glasses. Don't they make your eyes lazy?

A *I'm afraid this is a bit of a myth. While to a certain extent you do 'get used' to wearing glasses, it's a case of getting used to not straining in order to see and being able to read without effort. But if you hate the idea of having reading glasses, you're in luck – you can now get bifocal contact lenses, individually prescribed for each person's special combination of distance and near vision. It means that reading small print – as well as shifting focus between the road and a car's speedometer – becomes a lot easier.*

166

38

Get on yer bike

It's difficult to injure yourself cycling because it's such a low-impact form of exercise, plus it's a great way to tone your legs and the nicest way to see the countryside.

Cycling will also strengthen your heart, lower your blood pressure, boost your energy, burn off extra fat and reduce stress. So, what are you waiting for? Get on yer bike!

STRETCH IT OUT

Some cyclists, particularly those of you who hop on your bikes and cycle to work, rarely bother to warm up. If this is you, you might want to take a long hard look at your flexibility and posture. The main thigh muscle (the rectus femoris) has a high chance of being damaged unless you stretch it out properly. Another thing to watch out for is tight hamstrings and pulled hip flexors (at the top of the front of the thigh), which can happen often if you don't take time to stretch. A heel dig stretch might help as a basic exercise to help all three of these common muscle problems. Simply lift your toes, keeping your knee straight and your heel on the ground, until you feel a pull in the back and front of the calf and upper thigh.

Here's an idea for you...

If cycling gets your wheels turning consider combining it with a holiday. Find a company that'll give you an itinerary suited to your energy level plus accompanying cars to drop off your baggage at the next hotel on the route, then all you'll have to do is pedal and enjoy the view.

Hunching at the handlebars can lead to a permanent rounding of the shoulders and back. A typical yoga exercise can help counter act this – the Cobra. Lie on your front with your arms by your sides and lift your chest and head until you feel the movement in your back and shoulders. Don't forget to cool down properly too. Don't come to an abrupt halt, since your blood will pool in your legs. Instead, slow down gradually and finish with a few minutes of the heel dig stretch.

GETTING THE RIGHT BIKE FOR YOU

Your choice of bike depends on what you want your bike for. Mountain bikes are rarely suitable for riding in town and that goes for racing bikes too, however flash they may look. Having your head down when you ride is a sure way of going

headlong into a bus! If you've splashed out on a new bike, consider getting it sprayed with nasty black paint in order to stop other people thinking what a beautiful new bike you have and stealing it.

> '**There's no such thing as bad weather – only bad wet weather gear.**'
> A piece of traditional outdoor wisdom

Defining idea...

Swallow saddles (www.brooksengland.com) are back in vogue. These are long pointy saddles with an unfeasibly small sitting area that must owe more to aesthetics than to comfort as I imagine it's akin to sitting on a knife. I recommend looking at a seat that has a three-layered saddle of gel/foam/elastic that reduces pressure on the prostate and pubic bones (www.lookin.it). Aaah, that's more like it!

How did
it go?

Q   I'd love to cycle, but I'm terrified of being squashed by a car.

A   *Getting the right gear is paramount to making you feel safe. Wearing a
helmet is vital – most accidents on bikes resulting in serious injury involve
unnecessary head injuries. Also get yourself a bright fluorescent jacket or a
reflective strip. Back and front lights are the law, but make sure they're good
ones – it's all about being seen. Don't ride along hugging the curb, as this
will encourage cars to ignore you. Within reason, own your lane so that cars
have to make a conscious effort to pull out and pass you properly, like they
would another car, giving you plenty of space. When you're passing parked
cars, keep a particular eye out for people suddenly opening their car doors,
another good reason for allowing plenty of room around you when you ride.*

Q   I often consider cycling, but wet weather puts me off.

A   *Get some good lightweight waterproofs. Nowadays you don't have to look
like an angler expecting a force 12 gale as waterproofs are made of
extremely lightweight material, which folds up into a very small bundle.
(Peake do good gear.) Get both top and bottoms and even consider
waterproof shoe covers. Clear goggles are also a good idea, as they'll stop
water or stones being flicked up into your eyes. You might not look
beautiful with all this gear on, but you'll certainly be dry!*

39

It's not all in your mind

If you've gone off sex, it might be time to see your doctor.

Our bodies affect our libido much more than we'd care to admit.

It's an odd person that goes throughout life with the same level of sexual brio. Our income, lifestyle, confidence levels and any medication we've been prescribed by our doctor all affect how much desire we feel. But the big daddy that affects our libido is a hormonal change. Hormones determine so much about our lives, from how attractive we look (ovulating women get better looking) to the sorts of films we want to watch (new parents of both sexes have trouble with war movies).

This is why it's so odd that when we go off sex we don't head straight to the doctor for a check-up. What's even odder is how little use most of our doctors are if we actually do get there. I'm not getting at GPs, but they have limited resources and these tend to be focused on patients with cancer rather than those who only feel like sex once a month. So you'll have to do a lot of medical research yourself if you feel that your health is standing in the way of your love life. The internet is a wonderful thing, just don't start sending away for things that promise to make your penis bigger.

Here's an idea for you...

A lack of desire is one of the major symptoms of depression. It's also a side effect of some antidepressant drugs. What we call a catch-22. In cases of mild to moderate depression, exercise has been shown to be as effective as medication and might be well worth trying seriously.

We have very limited space, but this chapter is going to give you a few ideas to start you off on your own road to discovery vis-à-vis your body and provide you with some key words to type into the search engine. 'I want to have sex more' isn't a great thing to let Google know about, not unless you want a lot of strange men in Minneapolis trying to get friendly with you.

ARE YOU TAKING ANY MEDICATION?

If you are, you really do need to speak to your GP. Many different kinds of medication, including those for heart conditions and depression, can lower your libido. Some forms of the contraceptive pill also make you less interested in sex. Your GP may be able to change your prescription, but they won't be able to do that if you don't tell them there's a problem in the first place.

YOU'VE HAD A KID

The theory is that women go off sex so that they can concentrate on one baby's survival before conceiving another. My theory is that it's their own survival they're concerned about. Don't believe the books that tell you recovery only takes six weeks; but it doesn't take two years either. Having said that, many women do go off sex for literally years after giving birth – a weird physical and psychological inertia takes over. Eventually, you've just got to get back in the saddle and use every trick to rebuild your libido from the ground up.

If you're a man who's gone off sex big time since your child's been born, two things: you could be a terrific big-time bonder producing tons of a hormone that actually suppresses testosterone in new fathers, making you happy to hang around the metaphorical campfire with your missus and the little, un rather than, say, nipping to the cave next door for a bit of how's your father. In which case, your libido will come back. Alternatively, you could have deep-rooted psychological hang-ups along the Madonna/whore axis. In which case, you need therapy.

'I once made love for an hour and fifteen minutes. But it was the night the clocks were set ahead.'
GARY SHANDLING, American comedian

Defining idea...

YOU'RE OF A CERTAIN AGE

By this, I mean anything from about thirty-five on. For women, that's when the perimenopause kicks in – the period (no pun intended) leading up to the menopause proper. Your hormonal balance alters and although some women experience nothing at all, others are forgetful, moody, irritable and, of course, less interested in sex. Your GP may be able to prescribe HRT depending on your hormonal levels, but you may not be happy with this. There are a host of herbal remedies that can help maintain libido in the years up to and following the menopause. Try black cohosh and red clover.

How did it go?

Q   Do men have a male menopause?

A   *It seems that some do – the so-called andropause. So far, it's not been proven, but what has been found is that some men do respond to testosterone medication and regain their lust along with their love for life.*

Q   Would Viagra help me get my libido back?

A   *It might, but Viagra isn't completely without problems. One of the most obvious problems is that in a relationship where a man has had problems with arousal, his sudden priapic and demanding new persona can cause havoc. Read up on all the pros and cons and discuss it with your partner and doctor beforehand.*

Q   I've put on a lot of weight and thought that was the reason I was going off sex.

A   *It could be, but the weight gain might be a symptom of a condition that is robbing you of sexual desire. Low thyroid hormones is one possibility. So is diabetes or the menopause. Go to your doctor for a check-up and make sure you discuss your low libido as well as your weight gain.*

40

Does being overweight really matter?

Perhaps you never got back into shape after having kids or maybe you've always been a little plumper than you would like. How do you know if it's really a problem?

A very attractive, curvaceous woman in her early sixties once said to me, 'Darling, don't ever get too thin, it's so ageing.' And she was right!

I have friends who are in their early thirties and are incredibly proud of their skinny little size 8 or 10 frames, but look at least ten years older with their dried-up faces and flat little bottoms. I think a few curves and a couple of extra kilos are flattering and sensual – and that goes for men too.

When does a little plumpness become unacceptable? It depends on your viewpoint. If carrying a *few* extra kilos doesn't bother you, then it is not an issue. If it annoys you because you want to be in better shape, or it diminishes your confidence or stops you wearing the clothes you want to wear, then you should do something about it. If you have more than a few extra kilos, it does start to matter and when you're properly overweight it starts to matter very much indeed.

Here's an idea for you...

Get out your tape measure and calculator. Divide your waist measurement by your hip measurement (in centimetres). If the result is more than 0.95 for a man or 0.87 for a woman, you are apple-shaped. If you are apple-shaped, with more fat around your middle, your risk of heart disease is greater than if you're pear-shaped, with more fat on your bottom.

Fatness is a worldwide epidemic. In the UK alone, it is estimated that two-thirds of men and half of women are overweight, with one in five being obese, that is at least 12.5 kg (28 lb) overweight. Experts are predicting that one in four adults will be obese by 2010.

Obesity makes everyday life uncomfortable in so many ways, such as being unable to run for a bus, a lack of choice in clothes, rude stares and comments from other, thinner, people, and sleep and fertility problems. It is also the commonest cause of ill health and potentially fatal diseases. Obesity contributes to heart disease, diabetes, gallstones and some cancers. Just being overweight – and that's more than say a kilo or so – can raise your blood pressure and give you problems with cholesterol. Even dental decay is more common in overweight people.

In case you're in any doubt as to why being overweight does matter, here are some fat facts to consider:

According to the British Heart Foundation, heart and circulatory disease is the UK's biggest killer. Although the numbers are in fact slightly lower than twenty years ago, this is because of medical advances, not because we are getting healthier! There are other risk factors too, such as smoking, poor psychological health and inherited infirmities, but the truth is that 30% of deaths from coronary heart disease are directly linked to an unhealthy diet. The World Health Organisation estimates that somewhere between 1 and 24% of coronary heart disease is due to doing less than two and a half hours of moderate activity a week.

The fatter you are, the greater your risk. A weight gain of just 10 kg doubles your risk of heart disease. Reducing your weight even by 5 or 10% can have a beneficial effect on cholesterol levels.

Excess weight plays a part in high blood pressure, which can lead to blood clots, stroke and heart attacks. You can reduce these risks through diet: less salt, lower fat consumption and a huge increase in fruit and vegetable consumption.

Although the exact relationships are not fully understood, diet and cancer have an association too. A recent report suggested that as many as 40% of cancers have a dietary link. Breast cancer risk rises with a high fat diet or being overweight.

Clearly there's still a lot of research to be done, but it is certain that being overweight isn't fun and it isn't clever – and it can be about a lot more than the way you look.

'Imprisoned in every fat man a thin one is wildly signalling to be let out.'
CYRIL CONNOLLY

Defining idea...

How did it go?

Q   **I smoke and know I should give up, but I'm already overweight. I don't want to put on even more weight, which always happens when you quit. What shall I do?**

A   *Lots of people find that they put on up to 5 kg (10 lb) when they give up smoking. It's thought that nicotine somehow increases the metabolic rate. When you stop it lowers, which means if you eat the same amount, you will gain weight. Also when you first stop, you can't help snacking more (often out of boredom). This does tend to even out over a period of months. One way to keep weight gain down is to up your activity levels – as much as for distraction as burning up energy! Ultimately the benefits of not smoking have to be worth it. You could also try talking to your doctor about drugs, such as Zyban, that could help you quit without piling on the pounds.*

Q   **How does diet affect your cholesterol levels?**

A   *Firstly cholesterol isn't all bad, in fact it's needed by the body, but it's about the levels of the two kinds of cholesterol. HDL cholesterol is the good stuff, but LDL is the one you want less of. Trans fats (when liquid oils are hardened by hydrogenation in the manufacturing process) and saturated fats (found in meat, cream, butter, full fat milk and so on) cause LDL to rise, while fibre, vegetables and poly- and monounsaturated fats (think olive oil, sunflower oil and fish oils) not only lower LDL, but also boost levels of HDL cholesterol.*

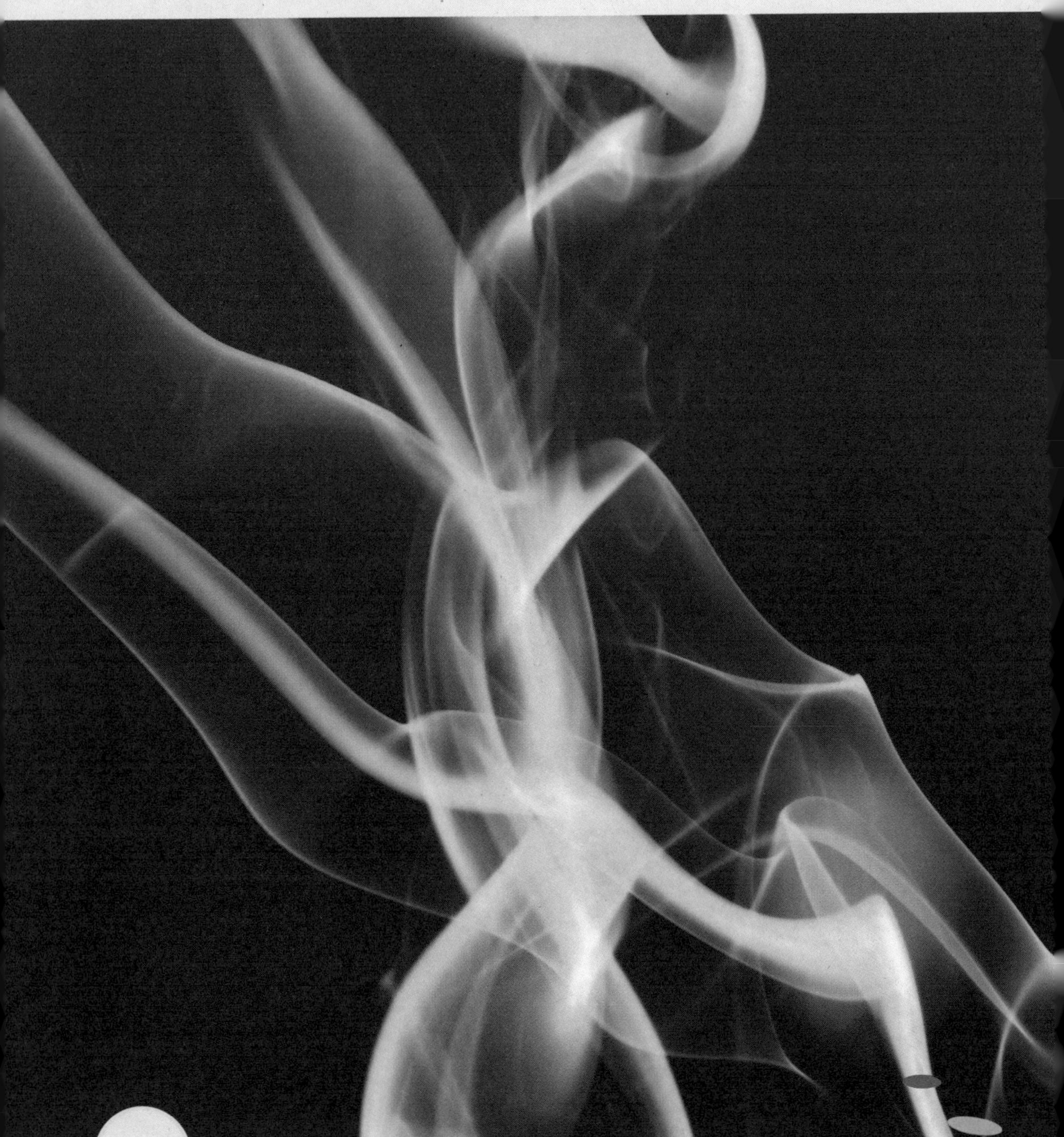

41

Slave to the weed

Let's face it – we are drug addicts. But nicotine, like many other drugs, is not a simple habit to crack. It's a collection of habits, triggered by certain events or actions in our day, each with its own battle to face.

Familiar patterns of behaviour are the smoke signals for our smoking demon who presses the button which triggers the reflex action to reach for the cigarette. Change the patterns, confuse the enemy and knock 'em dead one by one.

First of the day

Note the order you do things first thing in the morning. Change it. What do you have for breakfast? Change it. So, if your normal routine is dress, coffee and cigarette, then off to work – change to orange juice with the newspaper, then dress; or if it's cigarette, then tea and toast – change to listen to the radio over your cup of tea, and buy yourself some tasty jam or marmalade to jazz up your toast. Change the routine, disrupt the ritual triggers.

It has been said that if you smoke twenty a day but only start at midday you stand a better chance of stopping than someone who only smokes ten a day but lights up first thing.

If you can't give up all at once (cold turkey), delay that first cigarette of the day. Build up in blocks of ten or fifteen minutes each day.

On the way to work

If you drive, make a rule: no smoking in the car. Listen to the radio or take a music or talking book tape to listen to. If you live close to work, cycle or walk, remember not to take your cigarettes with you. If you take the bus or the train, take a newspaper or good novel and bury yourself in that. Make a rule: no smoking on the platform or in the bus queue.

Break time

Don't go outside with the smokers, follow the non-smokers' option. Change your drink if tea or coffee triggers the cigarette habit. Read your book, listen to music, find something practical to do with your hands.

Decide to stop – just like that. Don't smoke that last cigarette. Frame it in a sealed glass box and mount it somewhere prominent in the house.

The reward

Give yourself a drink or a snack. Decide on something pleasurable to buy yourself that doesn't involve tobacco and fire. Close your eyes and dream of your next holiday, or any other satisfying images. Make a phone call, take a stroll.

The stress reliever

Using techniques like yoga, meditation or visualisation is a much more effective way of relieving or at least managing stress. Ideally you should find a relaxing position for any of these techniques, but meditation exercises can be done almost anywhere – there will almost certainly be local classes available to teach you the basics.

Phone call

Don't have your cigarettes, lighter or an ashtray near the phone. Instead, make sure you have a pad and pen to doodle with. Answer the phone with the opposite hand to the one you usually use. If it's relevant, use your free hand to pick up a document.

After a meal

If at home, make the dining room a non-smoking zone. Enjoy a new drink after the meal as your pleasurable reward. If in a restaurant or cafe, ensure the table you have chosen is in a non-smoking area, and resist the temptation to go and stand out in the rain.

Work's over

Once again, change your routine, do something different. Go shopping, pick up some brochures for your next holiday, avoid going for a drink with colleagues, change your route home, think about the evening ahead, plan tomorrow – do anything different to distract your mind from its all-too-familiar paths.

With a drink

Choose a non-smoking pub or part of the bar (a lot easier these days), eat peanuts, play on the games machine, select some of your favourite music on the jukebox, sit outside and enjoy the wildlife, play cards, do a pub quiz and concentrate on the questions. Above all, try and choose non-smokers to drink with, and if you can't, don't be tempted into accepting a cigarette.

'Now the only thing I miss about sex is the cigarette afterward. Next to the first one in the morning, it's the best one of all. It tasted so good that even if I had been frigid I would have pretended otherwise just to be able to smoke it.'
FLORENCE KING

Defining idea...

'Coffee and tobacco are complete repose.'
Turkish proverb

Defining idea...

183

Last of the day

Distract yourself. Have a list of urgent jobs that need to be done around the home (we all have those), play with the children, take up a new hobby (particularly one that uses the hands). Set yourself an amount of time to do these activities in and the chances are you'll have passed the critical moment of the urge to smoke.

How did it go?

Q   **I enjoy going to the pub with my mates for a drink. The trouble is, they all smoke, and it feels unnatural not to join in, doesn't it?**

A   *The government may well lend a hand here. They've already done it in some countries like Ireland by banning smoking in public places. Lots of people still drink in Irish pubs but they don't smoke there any more. In the meantime, consider this – will your friends shun you forever if you choose not to smoke (and if they do, what kind of friends are they?)? And do you really want to be a victim of passive smoking without the rewards of smoking yourself?*

Q   **I have a very stressful job. My main reason for smoking is to chill out and restore a sense of calm. If I don't smoke I get really strung out and on edge. After work I use cigarettes to relax. If I didn't I'd make my partner's life hell – and she isn't going to put up with that. And why should she?**

A   *There are thousands of healthier ways to relieve stress and relax than smoking. Cigarettes are such a short-term fix and very inefficient. Try out some alternatives, whether it's yoga, long walks, worry beads, essential oils for a soothing bath. In fact, give them all a test drive until you find the ones that work for you.*

42

Steering clear of the 'big C'

Cancer is a scary word, but more than 90% of cancers are preventable.

Here are the easiest ways to cut your risk today.

There's been so much publicity about medical breakthroughs in the field of genetics in recent years, you could be forgiven for thinking that cancer is something you inherit and have no control over. But you're wrong; fewer than 10% of all cancers are linked to genetic inheritance. The rest are linked to lifestyle – something we all have control over.

Let's face it, cancer is a frightening subject that gets more scary as we get older and have a closer connection to the disease – family or friends who've experienced it. But to fight your enemy you must know it so here's a simple-to-understand guide to why cancer happens – and what you can do to reduce the risk.

Cancer is a simple term for a very complex condition. It begins with just one cell that suddenly begins growing, dividing and dividing again until it forms a tumour. If it becomes large enough or spreads, it can prevent the body's organs from working efficiently which, if left unchecked, can be fatal. One theory is that this abnormal growth is triggered not by a single factor, but by a number of factors coinciding – such as environmental exposure to hazards, a reduced immune system and genetic disposition.

Here's an idea for you...

Pucker up! Did you know that wearing lipstick reduces the risk of lip cancer by 50%? It's thought to be the reason why women have seven times less incidence of lip cancer than men. Ultraviolet light is a trigger for lip cancer and by applying lipstick, whether it contains an SPF or not, you block exposure to this. And who needs an excuse to look glamorous every day? Men, don't miss out – use protective lip salve.

Most of the body (99%) is made up of cells that continually grow, divide and then die. When each cell divides, it copies its DNA into the new cell. DNA is like your body's instruction book – it contains all the information it needs to keep your body alive. Problems begin when a mistake is made in the duplication process of the DNA, or when the DNA is damaged by an attacking free radical. In both cases, a mutation occurs which is then passed on when a cell divides. It's thought that trillions of these mutations occur in the body over a lifetime but that most of them don't matter. They're either harmless or so lethal that the cell is destroyed and doesn't get a chance to divide. But there is also a very rare third class of mutations that tell the cell to begin growing and dividing uncontrollably. At this point, a strong immune system will kick into action, root out the destructive cells and remove them – which is why strengthening your immune system is your best insurance against the big C.

Unfortunately, your chances of a cancer mutation slipping through the net increase with age simply due to the law of averages – the more divisions your cells undergo, the higher the likelihood that a cancer-causing mutation will occur. But experts also believe that cancer occurs when we're older because the immune system is weakened and simply less efficient. And although it may not sound like it, that's the good news – because there's much you can do to prevent the ageing of the immune system and keep it working at optimal capacity into your later years. Eating a diet high in fruit and vegetables (yes, it's that 'five a day' message again) is one of the easiest and most effective ways of doing this.

The other thing to bear in mind is that not all cancer kills. Some cancers are more harmful than others. Some cancers grow slowly, and cause little damage. The removal of a tumour, chemotherapy, radiation and other therapies can often stop cancer spreading. You could have a tumour removed in your thirties and live until your eighties.

At the risk of stating the glaringly obvious, prevention is better than cure when it comes to cancer. Your best chance of doing this is to avoid the known cancer-causing environmental factors such as smoking, obesity and poor nutrition as well as boosting the immune system so that it's better at detecting and destroying early cancers. And this can be as simple as not smoking, preventing stress, eating a healthy diet and doing some exercise on a regular basis. Now, what's scary about that?

'Since I came to the White House, I got two hearing aids, a colon operation, skin cancer, a prostate operation and I was shot. The damn thing is I've never felt better in my life.'
RONALD REAGAN

Defining idea...

How did it go?

Q **If one of my parents got cancer, does this mean I'm more likely to get it too?**

A   *Not necessarily. Genetics is thought to account for only 5% of cancer cases. Experts now believe that the majority of cases of cancer are lifestyle-related which means there is lots you can do to substantially reduce your risk. So try to stop worrying – nursing a parent through cancer is traumatic enough without the added stress of thinking that you're also going to get it.*

Q **What's the best way of surviving cancer if you do get it?**

A   *Early detection is the key. If a tumour is found and dealt with early, in 50% of cases, it won't recur. That's why it's vital that you keep up to date with your health checks. Women should get a smear test every three years and watch for changes in their breasts such as lumps or itchy patches. Men should check their testicles for lumps and consider asking their doctor for a prostate-specific antigen (PSA) test if they find they've been peeing more. You should both look out for changes in any moles, too.*

43

Upping the anti

Antioxidants could add years to your life by fighting free radical damage – if you're getting enough.

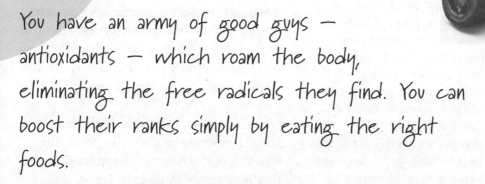

You have an army of good guys — antioxidants — which roam the body, eliminating the free radicals they find. You can boost their ranks simply by eating the right foods.

It's always important to know your enemy and in the war against ageing, it's free radicals, the unstable molecules that are a by-product of breathing and which damage the body's cells. There's nothing you can do to stop free radicals forming (except stop breathing, which would be a bit, well, radical), but antioxidants can eliminate them.

One half of the antioxidant army consists of compounds and enzymes that the body makes itself, using micronutrients found in the diet such as selenium, zinc, manganese, copper, iron, lipoic acid and glutathione. The other half are antioxidants delivered in the food we eat including vitamins A, C, E and B, and the vitamin-like compounds flavonoids, carotenoids and coenzyme Q10.

189

Here's an idea for you...

Black really is beautiful when it comes to staving off ageing. The darker the pigment – think plums, prunes, bilberries, blackberries, dates and raisins – the higher the ORAC rating. It's thought the pigment is a rich source of antioxidants. To maximise the benefits, wash rather than peel the skin of fruits and veg – the pigment is often concentrated in the skin or outer leaves. Try to eat a dark red, purple or black fruit or vegetable every day. And if you love wine, go for deep reds – they contain the most flavonoids.

When you eat a diet high in antioxidants, a protective shield is created around each cell which fights off and destroys the attacking free radicals. But if you're depleted in any of these micronutrients, there will be cracks in the shield. Many scientists believe the rise in heart disease, Alzheimer's and some cancers can be directly linked to micronutrient depletion. Our intake of selenium, for example, has fallen by 50% in the past fifty years due to intensive farming methods that leach it from the soil.

When it comes to their antioxidant content, not all foods were created equal. Meat, fish and dairy products do contain antioxidants but they're destroyed by cooking. Fruit and vegetables, however, contain high levels of antioxidants that survive the cooking process (as long as you don't boil them to mush). For very basic good health, you need 'five a day' – five portions (a portion is around a handful) of fresh fruit and vegetables a day. But to fend off ageing you need to step up a level and pack in as many antioxidants as possible.

It's easier to do than you might think, thanks to the brilliant scientists at Tufts University in the States who have very helpfully rated the antioxidant value of every food. It's a system known as ORAC: oxygen radical absorption capacity. The higher the ORAC, the more powerful a food is at mopping up free radicals.

'The amount of antioxidants that you maintain in your body is directly proportional to how long you will live.'
DR RICHARD CUTLER, anti-ageing researcher

Defining idea...

In fact, eating plenty of high-ORAC foods could raise the antioxidant power of blood by 10–25%.

One Tufts study of 1300 older people showed that those who had two or more portions a day of dark-pigmented vegetables such as kale and spinach were only half as likely to suffer a heart attack – and had a third of the risk of dying of cancer – compared with people averaging less than one portion a day. Other research has shown that a diet of high-ORAC foods fed to animals prevents long-term memory loss and improves learning capabilities. It may be no coincidence that this high-ORAC diet is very similar to the one eaten by the Hunza people of the Indian Himalayas, who commonly live beyond 100.

Visit your health-food store and you'll see you can buy antioxidants as a supplement. But the researchers at Tufts think it's the whole foodstuff and the way the hundreds of micronutrients within it (some of which they're yet to identify) react *together* that provides its powerful antioxidant punch. If you're the cautious type, take a belt-and-braces approach – aim for a high-ORAC diet and add a good antioxidant supplement just in case.

THE TOP ORAC-SCORING FOODS

The following figures are the number of ORACs that 100 grams of each food provides. A high-ORAC diet will provide 3000–5000 units a day.

Prunes, 5770
Raisins, 2830
Blueberries, 2400
Blackberries, 2036
Garlic, 1939
Kale, 1770
Cranberries, 1750
Strawberries, 1540
Spinach, 1260
Raspberries, 1220
Brussels sprouts, 980
Plums, 949
Alfalfa sprouts, 930

Broccoli, 890
Beetroot, 840
Avocado, 782
Oranges, 750
Red grapes, 739
Red peppers, 710
Cherries, 670
Kiwi fruit, 602
Baked beans, 503
Pink grapefruit, 483
Kidney beans, 460
Onion, 450
White grapes, 446

Q   I'm not sure about this – isn't it really complicated?

A   Try thinking of it as simply adding to your diet rather than completely changing it. Try a handful of prunes or blueberries on your breakfast cereal in the morning. Stuff some spinach leaves or avocado into your chicken roll for lunch. Add a side dish of steamed red cabbage and raisins with your main meal, and munch on a plum or some red grapes when you have a break.

Q   I only really like a few vegetables (potatoes, carrots and broccoli) but I do eat a lot of them. Am I getting enough ORACs?

A   It's a start. The bad news is that potatoes contain limited numbers of antioxidants so they aren't counted in your 'five a day'. You really need to widen your repertoire because different vegetables and fruits contain different micronutrients which all have a role to play. Antioxidant compounds are responsible for the bright colours of fruit and vegetables – from yellows, oranges and reds to purples, blues and greens. Your best anti-ageing insurance policy is really to try to eat a rainbow of colours every day to get the widest range of antioxidants. Why not be adventurous and buy something you've never tasted before? If you always eat broccoli, try spring greens instead. Swap sweet potatoes for ordinary potatoes, or add celeriac to your mash. Have you ever started the day with a berry smoothie or a fresh fig?

How did
it go?

44

Get organic

With more and more headlines screaming at us every day about unsafe food, is it any wonder that we're turning to organic food in our droves? But is it worth it?

From pesticide residue in pears to mercury poisoning from tuna, it's no wonder we're unsure about what's safe. But aside from this, we're turning to organic because of the taste. Remember how tomatoes should taste? Quite simply, like organic ones.

PRODUCTION MEANS PRIZES

Farmers have been under a huge amount of pressure to increase productivity, but at a cost. Many nonorganic fruit and vegetables contain a wide range of weedkillers, pesticides and fertilizers to increase food production. Fruit and vegetables also have to look perfect for supermarkets to accept them. Gnarled or pitted products are simply not accepted. But what effects do these chemicals have on human health? It seems that we know that pesticide residues can cause anxiety, hyperactivity,

Here's an idea for you...

If you can't afford to go the whole organic hog, then prioritise. The government advises that carrots, apples and pears should be peeled as they absorb insecticides through the skin, which could make them unsafe. Buying organic could be a better option. Conventionally farmed salmon are treated with pesticides to prevent mite infestations and there are fears that the chemicals become concentrated in the fish. And choose organic milk and beef, as 'normal' cows are in some countries treated with hormones and other growth promoters.

digestive problems and muscle weakness. Children are particularly vulnerable, as their immune systems aren't fully up and running and their comparatively small body mass means that chemicals are more concentrated.

And it's not just fruit and vegetables that we have to worry about. The biggest risks and the biggest worries come in the form of meat products: crazy cows, potty pigs – it's no joke. The many years of intensive farming in crowded conditions has reaped a whole host of health concerns. It's just not possible to crowd animals into such tight spaces without using industrial strength chemical agents to get rid of the threat of spreading disease.

FEEDING ON DEMAND

We're so used to having exotic fruit and vegetables out of season and on demand that at first it's difficult to accept that we can only get organic fruit and vegetables that are in season. Of course, a lot of organic food is produced abroad and flown to our supermarkets and this makes it more available, but vitamins and mineral content is lost if food has been on a long journey. It's therefore much better to buy locally produced products if you can. Many supermarkets are cottoning on to the fact that organic means *big* business. But remember that just because it says its

organic on the packet, it doesn't mean that it's better for you, especially if it has been processed. Once organic products have been turned into a crisp, cake or biscuit, for example, you'll have more or less the same concerns attached to the conventional versions of these foods: high sugar and fat.
So don't be had!

EXPECT THE INSPECTION

The term 'organic' is defined in law and can only be used by farmers who have an organic licence. These farmers have to follow guidelines on how to produce food to organic standards and they're inspected regularly to make sure that these standards are being met. Visit www.soilassociation.org to find out the ins and outs of organic certification in the UK.

Do I buy organic foods? Yes, and I think it's worth it. I always make sure that any meat, eggs or fish is organic and I get organic fruit and vegetables when they're available. I have a box delivered to my door. You'll probably find details of an organic home delivery company at your local healthfood shop. I'm now very aware of what fruit and vegetables are in season. And instead of looking in a recipe book and going out to buy what I need, I simply look in the box and create my menus around what I'm given.

'Organic farming delivers the highest quality, best-tasting food, produced without artificial chemicals or genetic modification and with respect for animal welfare and the environment, while helping to maintain the landscape and rural communities.'
PRINCE CHARLES, a big fan of organic food

Defining idea...

How did it go?

Q **I'm on a tight budget and organic food is too expensive. What can I do about all those pesticides?**

A *If you can't afford to buy organic, add a generous splash of vinegar to the water when you're giving your vegetables a scrub. There are also products that claim to remove pesticides from your fruit and vegetables – visit www.vegiwash.com to find out more.*

Q **Any other ways to save money?**

A *There are farmers' markets springing up everywhere. These are full of locally grown produce. All products sold are grown, reared, caught, pickled, baked, smoked or processed by the stallholder. Go at the end of the day, when the stallholders often sell produce more cheaply.*

45

Sleepy snacks

It's nearly time to hit the hay and you're not tired yet. Why not have a bedtime bite to kickstart those snooze hormones?

Many foods contain natural sedatives that stimulate the brain to produce calming chemicals which make you feel drowsy. Eat the wrong thing, though, and you could find yourself more awake than you were before.

A bedtime snack can not only help you drop off, it can stop you waking up in the middle of the night with a rumbling tummy. If you fall asleep easily but awaken several hours later, it may be due to low blood sugar – and a light bite before bed could nip that in the bud. You need to eat a high carbohydrate snack which has some fat just before you go to sleep. A banana works well as it digests slowly and helps your body release sleep hormones later in the night.

To help you go to sleep in the first place, you need something that's high in complex carbohydrates, with a small amount of protein which contains just enough tryptophan to relax the brain. A bit of calcium on top of this works a treat – it helps the brain use the tryptophan to make the sleep hormone melatonin. In fact the age-old sleep aid, a bowl of porridge, is probably the best sleep-inducing food of all as it

199

Here's an idea for you...

Instead of hot milk, make this oaty alternative. Soak a level tablespoon of oatmeal in milk for an hour or so in a small saucepan. Add a large glass of milk and bring to the boil gently, stirring all the time until it has slightly thickened. Pour it back into a glass, then add a spoonful of honey and plenty of grated nutmeg. You'll soon feel your eyelids get heavier and heavier ...

contains, complex carbohydrates, calcium and tryptophan. Some forty minutes later, your levels of melatonin will rise – setting you up for a deep, restorative sleep.

Avoid all-carbohydrate snacks, especially those high in junk sugars like biscuits – they're less likely to help you sleep. You'll miss out on the sleep-inducing effects of tryptophan, and you may set off the roller-coaster effect of plummeting blood sugar followed by the release of stress hormones that will keep you awake.

And yes, that old wives' tale about cheese before bed giving you nightmares is true. Cheese – particularly mature ones – contains the amino acid tyramine, which triggers the release of adrenaline. This stimulates your brain and can trigger vivid dreams as well as nightmares. The fat in cheese can also give you bad dreams – fatty food is more difficult to digest particularly when you're asleep as your digestive system automatically slows down. So while an army of enzymes tries to break down the fat, your sleep is being disrupted and you're dreaming of being chased by a giant piece of Brie.

RECIPES FOR SLEEP ...

Try one of these healthy snacks about forty minutes before you settle down under your duvet. This gives them enough time to perform their magic ...

- Honey with oatcakes
- Wholemeal toast with cottage cheese and pineapple
- Yoghurt and strawberries (yoghurt contains natural sleep-inducing substances called casomorphins)
- Three sticks of celery and low-fat fromage frais (celery contains a substance called 3-n-butyl phthalide, which acts as a gentle sedative)
- Banana slices and fromage frais
- Bagel with low-fat cream cheese and chopped dates
- Crackers and hummus
- Wholegrain cereal with milk
- Hazelnuts and tofu
- Peanut butter sandwich and ground sesame seeds – both of which contain tryptophan
- A few lettuce leaves– not a very exciting snack, but full of natural sedatives

'My favourite bedtime snack is Bran Flakes topped with maple and pecan muesli. Alternatively a Kit Kat – but they're strictly for midnight feasts only!'
ANNA FOSTER, morning breakfast radio show host

Defining idea...

If you fancy a snoozy bedtime drink to accompany your snack, then nothing beats a mug of warm milk and honey. But you can also try a milkshake made with skimmed milk, strawberries and low fat frozen yoghurt or a milkshake using soya milk (soya contains tryptophan). Alternatively, make your own herbal infusion from limeflower, lemon balm and lavender adding half a teaspoon of each to a mug of hot water. Cover (to prevent the plant oils evaporating), infuse for five minutes then sweeten with honey to taste.

How did
it go?

Q   Is it worth having a snack even if you've had a late dinner?

A   *Tryptophan works best on an empty stomach so your snack will have
maximum impact only if you've had dinner two or three hours earlier.*

Q   What about a tipple before bedtime?

A   *Under no circumstances drink alcohol before bed. It blocks tryptophan so all
the good effects of those sleepy snacks will go to waste.*

Q   Can you take these sleep hormones as supplements?

A   *Although they're not a substitute for a good diet and sound nutrition, some
experts still think they're a good way of boosting various sleep-promoting
substances. There are plenty of supplements available but in some countries
they're only available on prescription, not over the counter. As there have
been no published trials it's difficult to vouch for their effectiveness too. All
positive results are anecdotal. The supplement 5-HTP (5-hydroxytryptophan)
converts to serotonin in your body and is extracted from the seeds of a
West African plant. It's used for insomnia that's related to anxiety. L-
tryptophan is the pill form of tryptophan and there have been reports of it
raising levels of sleep-inducing melatonin by 300% in only ten minutes. It
should only be seen as a short-term measure, though. And melatonin
supplements, which are often taken for jet lag, can help insomnia – but
they don't have the mood-boosting benefits of the other two.*

46

The sex factor

People who have frequent sex live longer than those who don't.

We've known for a long time that a good relationship helps you live longer. Here's how to put the passion back into your life.

Men who are happily married live six years longer than single men. They're also far less likely to develop cardiovascular disease than unmarried men, even if their cholesterol levels are much higher. Women live around three years longer if they're married.

But it's not just marriage that's good for you. Now we know that a healthy sex life can keep you young. One study of 3500 people who looked on average ten years younger than their real age found that most were making love around three times a week (the average is around once a week). In fact, if you're a man and you have sex more than average, that is twice a week or more, you're far less likely to die from all causes than those men having sex once a week or less.

Here's an idea for you...

If your image of the typical sex-shop customer is a dodgy looking bloke in a grubby mac, you've obviously never been to one of the new ones springing up all over the place. They're full of great ideas for great nights in with your other half. Many are open in the evenings so why not visit one together on your next night out? If you really can't face it, or there isn't one near you, many of them have websites. Check out www.coco-de-mer.co.uk, for instance.

Not only is sex thought to be good exercise, improving cholesterol levels, increasing circulation and releasing endorphins, it may also release chemicals that benefit the immune system. Frequent ejaculations in men may reduce the risk of prostate cancer by as much as 33%.

It seems straightforward enough – have more sex if you want to live longer. Except that it's not just something you can simply add to the bottom of your daily 'to do' list ('ring accountant, sort out the shed, defrost supper, have sex'). If you've been in a relationship for several years you may be well past the 'ripping each other's clothes off' stage. Your body may be feeling the effects of both gravity and a bit of extra weight. That's normal and of course it doesn't mean you're no longer attractive. But it's easy to feel like that when you're surrounded by air-brushed images of nubile, scantily-clad sex goddesses (and gods) in the media, even if you do remember that the pictures are often doctored to make them look that good. So having sex more often is not just going to happen – you have to make it a bit of a project.

'Remember, if you smoke after sex, you're doing it too fast.'
WOODY ALLEN

Defining idea...

One of the main reasons we go off sex with our long-term partners is because there are so many distractions in life – paying the bills, doing the washing up, dealing with each other's families and the kids. Sex arises out of the quality of a relationship as a whole. To prioritise your sex life, you have to strengthen the whole relationship, of which sex is just a part. So forget the dishes, leave the answerphone on and sit down to pay each other some real attention. Make time to have a glass of wine and a chat together. Don't just talk practicalities, talk about your hopes and dreams. And make each other laugh!

Then put a little imagination into trying something new. It doesn't need to be superkinky – something as simple as scented massage oil and candlelight can work wonders. Experimenting is the best way of finding out what works for both of you. Now, when has homework ever been as much fun?

How did it go?

Q   Do old people really have sex?

A   *Yes, of course they do, lots of it, everywhere. Although if you believe the images we're fed by the media, the only people who ever have sex are under twenty-five and stunningly good-looking. But many couples find their sex life improves with age. A recent report found that 44% of the over-sixty-fives who were surveyed spent more than two hours a week making love. Another – of married and single men and women over sixty-five – found that most people described sex as being vital to their quality of life. Older women reported that one of the major reasons they believed sex became more pleasurable as they got older was because they no longer had to worry about contraception. Sex was also seen as a means of easing tension within marriage and as a wonderful tool for diffusing arguments, improving self-esteem, emotional well-being and body image. Pretty much the same as it is for younger couples, then.*

Q   My husband finds it a bit harder to perform these days. Should we try Viagra?

A   *Some sexual slowing down with age is natural and most men take longer to become aroused. It's a long way from impotence, but it can cause panic. Your husband may fear that he's going into a speedy sexual decline and will soon be unable to perform at all. In fact, some health conditions, such as diabetes or high blood pressure, can interfere with sexuality. It's usually temporary but there is a danger that 'performance anxiety' will take over, so the fear becomes a self-fulfilling prophecy. So above all, try to relax, and accept the changes. And don't try Viagra without first speaking to your doctor.*

47

Ready for a detox?

Detox is such a big buzz word these days, but what exactly does it mean?

In rebellion against the detox diet movement, someone I know did a retox diet during the football season. His method was to drink several pints of lager. The media remind us daily how all the stars have detoxed, but what does this involve?

Doing a detox diet isn't quite as simple as you might think. What detox actually means to you really depends on where you are with your diet now. If you're drinking lots of alcohol, simply eliminating the booze for a few days might constitute a detox diet. To someone who already has quite a pure diet, however, eliminating wheat and dairy might be a detox. Taking stock of where you are is important because if you detox too quickly you could experience a number of unpleasant symptoms, such as headaches, lack of energy and generally feeling unwell. Don't think of doing a detox when you have an important week at work, as you might have a bit of a fuzzy head.

Here's an idea for you... Get a juicer and start making your own juice. You might like to try a combination of apple and blueberry or carrot and apple. Juices can be full of vitamins and minerals that help the detoxification systems important to the body. But remember to use organic fruit as there are pesticides on conventionally grown fruit.

DON'T MAKE ME

Why should we put ourselves through a detox? Isn't it really hard work? Our bodies are in a constant state of renewal at cell level, but if there's an overload of toxins either from food or environmental sources our bodies struggle to deal with them, effectively putting a strain on the kidneys and liver and taking away energy that could otherwise be used for living. A detox diet allows us to stop overloading the body with harmful substances and, if we give the body plenty of the right nutrients, it can speed up the elimination of toxins and promote cell renewal.

WARM-UP

If you're afraid of becoming Mr or Mrs Fuzzy Potatohead, then the thing to do is to start slowly over a period of one month. Choose in the first week to eliminate coffee, chocolate and caffeine drinks (cola drinks), replacing them with lots of water and herbal teas. In the second week, try eliminating wheat products (cakes, biscuits, pasta) and substitute them with rye bread or other grains such as brown rice, quinoa, buckwheat or millet. In the third week, try substituting dairy products for sheep and goat products. And in the fourth week, increase your water intake up to at least 2 litres (3.5 pints) of water a day, while avoiding alcohol.

You might want to take into consideration environmental toxins too and try to avoid them during this period. Are you a smoker? Do you regularly use aerosol sprays? Do you take lots of over-the-counter medication (for example, for headaches)? What about your exposure to traffic fumes? If you're a cyclist, consider wearing a mask to filter fumes.

'The world is round and the place which may seem like the end may also be the beginning.'
IVY BAKER PRIEST

Defining
idea...

How did it go?

Q   **I want to go a little further with my detoxing. Any suggestions?**

A   *Start with the warm-up described above so that when you take it a step further you don't experience unpleasant reactions. Then keep avoiding wheat, alcohol, dairy products and caffeine. Take a week off work if possible and really indulge in your experience. Go shopping and get prepared before you start. You'll need lots of fresh fruit, including lots of lemons, and vegetables. Also, get some vegetable juices (beetroot or carrot are good, but not tomato), millet (an alkaline grain and very detoxifying) and brown rice. If your budget can run to it add in a good antioxidant supplement (advanced antioxidant solgar would be good), some flax seeds and a green superfood (try Kiki's E3 Live or Nature's Living Superfood from www.kiki-health.com). Start your day with a drink of hot water and lemon juice and do some yoga or stretching exercises if possible. Breakfast should be millet porridge made with water, with some fruit and berries added. Intersperse your day with plenty of water and herbal teas. Lunch should be a huge salad that includes many colours – greens, oranges and reds. Dinner should be steamed vegetables and a small portion of brown rice. Before bed, do a breathing exercise. See how wonderful you feel in a week. Take plenty of rest in the first few days – you could get a cleansing reaction where you feel below par, but it will pass.*

Q   **How often should you detox?**

A   *I choose to detox at the beginning of each of the four seasons. Some people use Sundays to do a mini detox where they eat lighter or even do a juice fast where they drink vegetable juice (not tomato) throughout the day and finish with lightly steamed vegetables in the evening.*

48

Off the bus, up the stairs

Not getting any exercise because you're stuck in front of the computer all day? Did you know it's possible to exercise during the working day without even thinking about it?

Just take a moment to think about your typical workday. You get up, use the bathroom, hopefully you eat breakfast, you get the kids off to school.

You read the morning paper at breakfast or on your way to work. The bus, train or car transports you, and when you arrive perhaps you climb into the lift. You make a coffee in the staff kitchen, and then switch on your computer or whatever equipment you use. OK, so this may not exactly be your start to your workday but it's probably close enough.

Ask people why they don't exercise on workdays and the usual response is that they just don't have the time: we're working for longer hours, with greater workloads and to tighter deadlines. Now experts recommend doing thirty minutes of moderately intense physical activity on at least five days of the week to help reduce the risk of health problems such as high blood pressure. Like algebra (remember

Here's an idea for you...

You probably have meetings every now and then at work. You may have them every day. If you are having a meeting, or even just gossiping, with one or two other colleagues, rather than sitting around a table or standing still, try walking while you are talking.

algebra?), at first glance this time and motion equation doesn't seem to work. But there are solutions.

To begin with the thirty minutes doesn't have to be all in one go. It can be fifteen-minute, ten-minute or even five-minute blocks. It doesn't need to be exercise as such. It's activity that is important. Getting up and going to see a colleague rather than sending an email, going to a local coffee shop to get your mid-morning coffee rather than making it in the staff kitchen, these all count towards the thirty minutes of activity. You don't need to be sweating and panting, you just need to feel warm, slightly out of breath and for your heartbeat to increase.

So let's return to your workday routine, because this is the key, making these beneficial activities part of your routine.

At each stage of your day think about how you can change what you are doing so that you are more active doing it. For example, instead of having your morning newspaper delivered, walk to the newsagent and buy it. Perhaps you could walk with your children to school. They'll certainly benefit from this. Could you walk or cycle to work? If not, think about getting off the bus one stop earlier and walking the rest of the way. Use the stairs rather than the lift, or if you don't need the lift take a slightly longer route to your work area. Each time you have to use the stairs go up and down twice instead of just once. You'll soon feel your heart rate increasing when you do this. Rather than leaning just propping up the

'A man's health can be judged by which he takes two at a time – pills or stairs.'
JOAN WELSH

Defining idea...

photocopier, walk to and from your desk while it's churning out those vital documents. Try taking a slightly longer route to the copier, and walk briskly. These all count. Amazing isn't it. In fact, by lunchtime you could have already done your thirty minutes.

Although many people seem to be able to go all day without using the bathroom, again because they are too busy, the reality is we all need to go during the day. So try this. When you need to use the bathroom, if possible use one on a different floor to the one you usually use, or use one that is further away – you may want to practise this during times when you don't need to go so that you don't get caught short. You could also try going to the bathroom every one to two hours, whether you feel the need to go or not. You see, if you walk briskly there and back you could easily be achieving 25% of the day's activity requirement, doing something you should be doing anyway.

How did it go?

Q **We don't have a local coffee shop, and anyway my boss doesn't like employees to leave the building. How can I turn my caffeine fix into an activity?**

A   *OK, but I presume your boss doesn't mind you having a coffee or tea break. Here's what you do. Take a longer route to the kitchen. Ask colleagues if you can make them a cup, but don't phone or email them, actually walk and do the rounds collecting the orders. While the kettle is boiling, jog on the spot or walk briskly around the workplace, maybe walk up and down the stairs. You see, you can be active during time that you would probably have been standing still, time that your boss accepts you need to have away from your workstation. What you are doing is making good use of the time.*

Q **I'm always running late for work. How can I find the time to do these things in the morning?**

A   *I'm guessing that getting up a little bit earlier to create some time is not possible for you? You can be more active during the day in the ways we've already talked about. Moreover, if it's hard for you to do these things at the beginning of the day, do them at the end of the day. Use the stairs when you leave work, don't get on the bus at your usual stop but walk to the next stop, and also get off one stop earlier. If you drive to work, then park your car further from your workplace than you would normally do.*

49

Is stress making you fat?

Any sort of stress can lead to weight gain.

Stress causes your body to release cortisol and this stimulates the fat-storing hormone, insulin. Insulin causes your body to hold on to its fat stores.

And that's if you're eating what you always ate. The trouble is that you might be sabotaging yourself without realising it. When we're stressed there's a tendency to overeat, especially carbohydrates. (It's not called comfort food for nothing.) That's because carbohydrates cause the brain to release serotonin and this is one of the feel-good hormones that raise mood. In a way, it's a form of self-medication.

As is booze. Terrific at relaxing you. Fabulous for adding layers of fat around your waistline.

STAY SVELTE EVEN WHEN STRESSED

It's not what you eat it's when you eat it.

Researchers discovered that when women ate 'off piste' – whenever they wanted – they ate 120 calories a day more than those women who ate three meals and three snacks a day at set times. Decide on your meal times and stick to them. No grazing.

Here's an idea for you...

When you're stressed and feel the temptation to reach for comfort food, try sucking on half a teaspoon of honey instead (manuka honey from New Zealand is especially beneficial). Honey causes the brain to release the feel-good hormone serotonin almost immediately. You might find that just that tiny amount will satisfy you and prevent you pigging out on a bar of chocolate or a packet of biscuits which also cause serotonin release but pack a lot more calories.

Make a conscious effort to cut out salt

We can feel more drawn to salty foods when we're stressed. There could be a physiological reason for this. Salt raises blood pressure and that in turn actually raises cortisol levels – which might have been an advantage when we only got stressed once a month but is redundant for the most part now. Wean yourself from adding salt to food and aim to eat no more than 6 g of salt a day in processed food. If the levels are given in sodium then multiply by 2.5 to get the grams of salt.

Get into green tea

Caffeine raises levels of stress hormones and makes you even more stressed. Try green tea. It has about half the caffeine of coffee and a little less than black tea. And it's good for your brain and your circulation as well as your waistline. There's another advantage. A recent Japanese study found that people drinking green tea lost 2.4 kg (5.3 lb) after three months, while those who drank black tea lost only 1.3 kg (2.9 lb). It's also thought that chemicals called catechins found in green tea trigger weight loss.

Savour food

Apparently, it takes twenty minutes for our stomach to register that we've started to eat and switch off the feeling of hunger. It's certainly borne out by a small US study of women who were instructed to eat slowly, chewing each mouthful carefully, savouring their food. These women were told to stop eating when their most recent bite didn't taste as good as the first. They lost 3.6 kg (8 lb). In the same period of time, the control group gained 1.3 kg (3 lb). Our bodies know when we've had enough if we slow down long enough to listen.

> '*My doctor told me to stop having intimate dinners for four, unless there are three other people.*'
> ORSON WELLES

Defining idea...

Relax

One study showed that women who made a conscious effort to relax lost an average of 4.5 kg (10 lb) in eighteen months without consciously dieting. The truth is you need actively to relax in order to switch off the stress hormones which could be contributing to weight gain.

Compete with yourself

The best possible antidote to stress *and* weight gain is to exercise. Buy a pedometer from a sports shop. Measure how many steps you take in an average day (most people average around 4000), and then do a few more steps each day until you reach 10,000.

How did it go?

Q   I've got more than 10 kg to lose. Green tea isn't going to cut it. Any suggestions?

A   *Look at the South Beach Diet, created by Dr Arthur Agatston, a genuine bloke who developed his diet to help his heart patients – not to make a fast buck (although he must be pretty glad he did). This is the most successful diet I've come across and works for people who don't 'do' diets (including my mother who has lost tons of middle-age spread and returned to the svelte figure of her youth with this diet). The basic principle is a hybrid of the glycaemic index (GI) diet and Atkins (but healthy). You cut out carbohydrates for the first two weeks – no bread, pasta, sugar, fruit – and no booze. You eat meat, fish, eggs, cheese and vegetables. After two weeks you start reintroducing a few 'good' carbohydrates, notably fruit, and a glass or two of wine (he's a cardiologist and he's big on red wine) but the good thing is that cravings for the carbohydrate foods which most experts think contribute to weight gain if we eat them in excess diminish rapidly. Weight comes off easily.*

Q   I've tried your ideas. I'm eating healthily. I'm still gaining weight. What else can I try?

A   *How are you sleeping? If you're not sleeping well, you need to look at that, too. Doctors are only beginning to understand the connection between stress and sleep patterns. Several recent studies have found a link between obesity and sleeping fewer hours than average. It's counterintuitive: one would think those that are awake longer would be burning off calories like billie-oh, but it's not the case. Several other studies indicate much the same outcome. This research is in its infancy, but if you are sleeping badly, accept it might be affecting your metabolism.*

50

The veggie question

Studies show that vegetarians live longer and suffer less heart disease and cancer. Is it time to ditch the meat?

If you're a vegetarian, it's time to feel smug. You're already a winner when it comes to anti-ageing.

You can look forward to ten extra years of disease-free living than meat-eaters and you're 39% less likely to die from cancer. You're also 30% less likely to die of heart disease.

Anti-ageing scientists think meat doesn't do you many favours – and they point to the world's longest-lived communities to prove it. A famous study called the China Project highlighted the difference between mainly vegetarian Chinese from rural areas, who stay disease-free late into life, and their meat-eating urban counterparts who succumb to heart disease, stroke, osteoporosis, diabetes and cancer.

But hang on, you're thinking, if we're designed to munch plant food only, how come our cavemen ancestors ate meat? It's a good point. Trouble is, although the human race did evolve as omnivores, we now eat more meat in a week than our ancestors did in months. Obviously, this is partly because we no longer have to chase our meat with a spear before eating it. But it's also due to changes in farming

Here's an idea for you...

It's a myth that meat is the best source of protein – it's also found in some surprising foods, like brown rice for instance. Add a small tin of mixed beans (rinse them in a sieve under the tap first) to cooked, cooled brown rice and sprinkle with a few drops of sesame oil to taste. Garnish with fresh coriander and you've got a delicious, anti-ageing salad that contains all eight of the vital amino acids that protein supplies.

patterns that mean meat and dairy products are cheaper and more readily available than ever before.

If you're tucking into a burger right now, you may want to read the following paragraphs some other time. There's a theory that humans have a long colon, like a horse or cow, and a relatively slow food transit designed to break down grains and grasses. Too much meat introduced into the system literally rots before it reaches the end, releasing toxins into the bloodstream.

Dr Colin Campbell, chairman of the World Cancer Research Fund, believes 'animal protein is one of the most toxic nutrients there is' and that 'the vast majority, perhaps 80 to 90%, of all cancers, cardiovascular diseases and other forms of degenerative illness can be prevented, at least until very old age, simply by adopting a plant-based diet'. Still eating that burger? The theory is that animal fats are high in saturated fats which raise levels of bad (LDL) cholesterol, increasing the risk of heart disease. Vegetarians, by contrast, tend to eat a lot of plant-based foods which are high in disease-fighting antioxidants.

Most meat-eaters also eat too much protein (even those who aren't on the Atkins diet). According to the World Health Organisation, we need around 35 g of protein a day, but the average meat-eating woman eats around 65 g

'It always seems to me that man was not born to be a carnivore.'
ALBERT EINSTEIN

Defining idea...

and the average man, 90 g. We do need to eat some protein with every meal but you don't always have to add meat to ensure you get it. If your meal contains fish, lentils and beans, grains like rice, quinoa and bulgar wheat, eggs, yogurt, cheese, nuts or seeds, you're probably already eating enough.

But what if you're a diehard meat fan who can't bear the thought of life without a Sunday roast? Don't despair – omnivores who eat above average amounts of fruit and vegetables can cut their risk of most cancers by 50–75%. And by increasing the amount of plant foods you eat, you'll probably find you naturally cut back on meat consumption.

How did it go?

Q   **I'm a big bloke. Don't I need the protein from meat to keep me going?**

A   *Are you heavier than the average male gorilla? They weigh in at nearly 400 kg (800 lb) which they happily sustain on a diet of vegetables, fruits and nuts. Many top sports nutritionists now recommend a vegetarian diet as the best way of building lean muscle tissue.*

Q   **If I can't live without meat, which are the healthiest choices to opt for?**

A   *Most nutritionists recommend switching from red meat to white meat, as that contains the less saturated fats. In Mediterranean countries red meat is seen as a treat for a couple of times a month. Skinless turkey breast is one of the leanest meats available, and it's also a good source of cancer-fighting selenium and zinc, which boosts the immune system. Chicken breast is also a good choice. If you can afford it, opt for organic meat which doesn't contain growth hormones and antibiotics. The very worst options are processed meats such as hot dogs, burgers and cured meats as they contain high amounts of nitrates which are thought to be carcinogenic. (In one study of 30,000 older women, those who ate a lot of hamburgers had twice the normal risk of certain kinds of cancer.) Char-grilled meat is also thought to be high in carcinogenic compounds known as HCAs – try stir-frying strips of meat instead.*

51

Build a better baby

Diet and nutrition for pregnancy. Does a little of what you fancy really do you good?

'You are what you eat' has never been a truer statement than in pregnancy. You are creating a whole new person — and you want to make the fuel you provide for this amazing process the best you possibly can. But does that mean goodbye to your favourite treats?

The simple answer is no. While it's important to make sure you are well nourished during your pregnancy, that does not mean you have to don a hair shirt and sign up for a life of abstention! If you were eating a largely healthy diet before you became pregnant, you won't need to make drastic changes.

Ensure you are eating a broad range of food encompassing all the food groups – and no, chocolate is not a food group – grain products, vegetables, fruits, protein foods and dairy products. By eating well you can make sure that your baby gets everything they need as they grow for maximum brain and body development.

Here's an idea for you...

Buy a notebook and keep a 'food log' if you're having problems with your diet. It will help you to have an overview to make sure you are eating enough of the right foods.

PACK IN THE PROTEIN!

A pregnant woman needs 75–80 g of protein a day. Hard cheeses are a great source of protein. So are lean meat, cooked fish, pulses, cow's milk, soya beans and eggs. Protein is the building block for human cells – and that includes your baby, as well as a large part of you! Your muscles, cartilage, tendons, bone, skin and hair are all mainly made from types of protein.

Avoid blue-veined cheese, mould-ripened soft cheese such as brie, and soft, unpasteurised cheese made from goat's or sheep's milk due to the risk of listeria, a type of food poisoning very dangerous in pregnancy.

CRANK UP THE CALCIUM

Calcium is vital for the development of muscles and nerves, blood clotting and enzyme activity. It is needed for building strong bones and teeth – and bone strength for you, if you don't want to end up with osteoporosis.

Adult women need around 1000 mg of calcium a day, and pregnant women need a little more. Semi-skimmed or skimmed milk is a great source of calcium. One glass of milk provides about 300 mg of calcium. Other good sources are cottage cheese, yoghurt, sardines and salmon, collard greens and kale, corn tortillas and firm tofu. Blackstrap molasses is a great source – I developed a strange craving for two large sticky dollops in hot milk when I was pregnant with number two. I hate hot milk. I guess the baby didn't...

LOAD THOSE COMPLEX CARBS

Complex carbohydrates will give you a great source of slow burn energy, and will help you to avoid 'pregnancy fatigue'. Carbohydrates also help to prevent constipation – you'll be 'pushing through your bottom' soon enough, thanks.

Choose whole-grain or fortified products such as whole-wheat bread, cereal, pasta and rice. Beans and peas, fresh fruit and vegetables are also good sources of carbohydrates. Include as many unrefined carbohydrates as you can – the less processing the better. That doesn't mean you have to chew on crispbreads that taste like old board. Choose a crunchy wholemeal roll smothered in seeds instead.

VITAL VITAMINS

Other important nutrients you should consume via foods in pregnancy include vitamin D, iron, vitamin B12, zinc and folic acid.

Your vitamin B12 needs are higher in pregnancy due to vitamin B12's role in tissue creation and the building of DNA – and you're making a whole new person! The recommended daily allowance (RDA) for vitamin B12 in pregnancy is 2.2 micrograms. A rounded teaspoon of yeast powder provides 2.2 micrograms of vitamin B12, which you can stir into a glass of orange juice. Although that gets it over in one go, I tried it with baby number one and it made me want to vomit.

'When pregnant women are severely undernourished, their children can be born with fewer than half the brain-cells of a healthy child.'
GORDON DRYDEN and DR JEANNETTE VOS, *The Learning Revolution*

Defining idea...

Happily, an alternative source of vitamin B12 is fortified cereal. Meat, dairy products and eggs are also good sources of B12, and fermented soya products such as tempeh, miso, shoyu and tamari, as well as seaweed have been suggested as vegan alternatives.

Good sources of vitamin C include fruits and vegetables such as oranges, strawberries, tomatoes, peppers, raspberries and cabbage.

You must include iron-rich foods in your diet. Your baby needs iron for the development of its blood supply. Foods that are high in iron include cashew or pistachio nuts, carob, lean beef, pulses, fresh parsley and wholewheat cereals. Drinking orange juice, containing vitamin C, will help you to absorb the iron in your food more readily.

FABULOUS FATS

Make sure you consume enough essential fatty acids (EFAs) such as found in oily fish as they help the development of your baby's brain. Your mother was right: fish is 'brain food'! Walnuts, wholegrains, green leafy vegetables and rapeseed oil are also good sources.

Q **I usually drink plenty of water to keep my skin clear. Do I need to drink more now that I'm pregnant?**

How did it go?

A *The volume of fluids in your body increases during pregnancy, and so does your need for fluid intake. Drink at least six to eight large glasses of water a day – and more if it's hot. Keeping well hydrated has many benefits including clear skin, no constipation, and it will reduce the risk of water retention and urinary tract infections.*

Q **I have a real craving for crisps and salty snacks. Will they harm me or my baby?**

A *Too much salt in pregnancy may increase your blood pressure, which has health implications for you and your baby. Try to substitute other savoury snacks, such as vegetable crudités or cheese for the crisps.*

52

Are you younger than you think?

Take this quiz and find out your true biological age.

Ever told a tiny white lie and knocked off a few years when someone asks you how old you are? You may be being more honest than you think.

Scientists believe that as well as a calendar age, you also have a biological or 'body' age, which is determined by your health and lifestyle. We all know people who seem younger than their years – and those who seem old before their time. Now scientists believe that it's possible to have a biological age or body age of fifty in our seventies. We're only just realising that how fast, or how slowly, we age is a process that's under our control. We now know that our diet, activity levels, and even our emotional health all have a direct effect on the ageing process. How long your body and mind stay fit, active and healthy is determined by how you live your life.

It's only a matter of time before scientists devise a definitive method of determining true body age. And who knows, in the future, perhaps we'll come to discard birth dates altogether and use personal age assessments instead for employers, insurers – maybe even dating agencies!

Here's an idea for you…

The static balance test is an instant way of assessing your biological age. Stand barefoot on a flat surface with your feet together and your eyes closed. Raise your right foot six inches off the ground (if you're left-handed, raise your left foot). See how many seconds you can maintain your balance without having to open your eyes or put your foot down. Here are the approximate values (time in seconds before falling over) for different biological ages.

- 04 seconds – 70 years
- 05 seconds – 65 years
- 07 seconds – 60 years
- 08 seconds – 55 years
- 09 seconds – 50 years
- 12 seconds – 45 years
- 16 seconds – 40 years

In the meantime, try the quiz below to find out how you're ageing so far. Don't be dismayed if it's not good news. There's plenty of information to help you knock years off your true age and keep your biological age as young as possible.

WHAT'S YOUR BODY AGE?

Start with your calendar age. If you can answer 'yes' to any of the following questions, add or subtract years as directed to find your body age.

1. Do you get at least thirty minutes of moderate exercise (like walking) on most days?
   YES – subtract 1 year

2. Do you exercise really intensively on a regular basis?
   YES – add 3 years

3. Do you rarely, if ever, do any physical exercise?
YES – add 2 years

4. Are you more than 10% over the recommended weight for your height?
YES – add 3 years

5. Are you the correct weight for your height?
YES – subtract 1 year

6. Are you under stress or pressure on a regular basis?
YES – add 4 years

7. Do you actively practise stress-reducing techniques such as meditation or yoga?
YES – subtract 3 years

8. Have you experienced three or more stressful life events in the past year
(for example divorce, bereavement, job loss, moving house)?
YES – add 3 years

9. Do you smoke?
YES – add 6 years

*'I was wise enough to never
grow up while fooling most
people into believing I had.'*
MARGARET MEAD, anthropologist

*Defining
idea...*

10. Do you have a cholesterol level of 6.7 or higher?
    YES – add 2 years

11. Do you have blood pressure that's 135/95 or over?
    YES – add 3 years

12. Do you eat five or more portions of a range of fresh fruit and vegetables every day?
    YES – subtract 5 years

13. Do you regularly eat processed, packaged or fast food?
    YES – add 4 years

14. Are you a vegetarian?
    YES – subtract 2 years

15. Do you eat oily fish three times a week?
    YES – subtract 2 years

16. Do you drink two or three small glasses of red wine, up to five days a week?
    YES – subtract 3 years

17. Do you drink more than 21 units of alcohol a week (if you're a man) or 14 (if you're a woman)?
    YES – add 5 years

18. Do you have an active social life and a supportive network of friends and family?
    YES – subtract 2 years

19. Do you have an active sex life?
    YES – subtract 2 years

20. Are you happily married?
    YES – subtract 1.5 years.

Q   I'm a bit worried – I'm five years older than I thought I was. What should I do?

How did it go?

A   *Don't worry. Lowering your biological age is easier than you think – all it takes is some simple lifestyle changes. And I mean simple: could you handle drinking more tea, flossing your teeth and learning a new hobby? They'll all make you biologically younger. OK, there are some changes that require more effort, such as changing your diet, losing weight and exercising more, but you don't have to make every change at once. Take one step at a time and you'll soon see results.*

Q   Great – I'm much younger than my calendar age. Can I take it easy then?

A   *Well done! You're obviously already doing lots of the right stuff – eating plenty of fresh fruit and veg, getting some moderate exercise and avoiding stress. But don't rest on your laurels; now's the time to consolidate all your good work and ensure you have years of health and vitality ahead.*

233

The end...

Or is it a new beginning? We hope that the ideas in this book will have inspired you to try some new things to improve your health. You've discovered that by making small changes to your diet and exercise routine and taking a good look at your bad habits you've begun to feel better. Hopefully the tips you read here will help you to continue on the path to a long and healthy life.

So why not let *us* know all about it? Tell us how you got on. What did it for you – what really improved your wellbeing? Maybe you've got some tips of your own you want to share (see next page if so). And if you liked this book you may find we have even more brilliant ideas that could change other areas of your life for the better.

You'll find the Infinite Ideas crew waiting for you online at www.infideas.com.

Or if you prefer to write, then send your letters to:
The best value health book ever
The Infinite Ideas Company Ltd
36 St Giles, Oxford OX1 3LD, United Kingdom

We want to know what you think, because we're all working on making our lives better too. Give us your feedback and you could win a copy of another *52 Brilliant Ideas* book of your choice. Or maybe get a crack at writing your own.

Good luck. Be brilliant.

Offer one

CASH IN YOUR IDEAS

We hope you enjoy this book. We hope it inspires, amuses, educates and entertains you. But we don't assume that you're a novice, or that this is the first book that you've bought on the subject. You've got ideas of your own. Maybe our author has missed an idea that you use successfully. If so, why not send it to yourauthormissedatrick@infideas.com, and if we like it we'll post it on our bulletin board. Better still, if your idea makes it into print we'll send you four books of your choice or the cash equivalent. You'll be fully credited so that everyone knows you've had another Brilliant Idea.

Offer two

HOW COULD YOU REFUSE?

Amazing discounts on bulk quantities of Infinite Ideas books are available to corporations, professional associations and other organisations.

For details call us on:
+44 (0)1865 514888
Fax: +44 (0)1865 514777
or e-mail: info@infideas.com

235

Where it's at...

brilliant ideas

The Best Value Ever Series is published by Infinite Ideas, publishers of the acclaimed **52 Brilliant Ideas** series and a range of other titles which are all life-enhancing and entertaining. If you found this book of interest, you may want to take advantage of this special offer. Choose any two books from the selection below and you'll get one of them free of charge*. See p. 242 for prices and details on how to place your order.

Goddess
Be the woman YOU want to be Edited by Elisabeth Wilson
BUMPER BOOK – CONTAINS 149 IDEAS!

Healthy cooking for Children
52 brilliant ideas to dump the junk
By Mandy Francis

Adventure sports
52 brilliant ideas for taking yourself to the limit
By Steve Shipside

Skiing and snowboarding
52 brilliant ideas for fun on the slopes
By Cathy Struthers

Getting away with it
Shortcuts to the things you don't really deserve
Compiled by Steve Shipside

Re-energise your sex life (2nd edition)
52 brilliant ideas to put the zing back into your lovemaking
By Elisabeth Wilson

* If books vary in price we'll supply the lowest priced one free.
Postage at £2.75 per delivery address is additional.

Stress proof your life
52 brilliant ideas for taking control
By Elisabeth Wilson

Upgrade your brain
52 brilliant ideas for everyday genius
By John Middleton

Inspired creative writing
Secrets of the master wordsmiths
By Alexander Gordon Smith

Detox your finances
Secrets of personal finance success
By John Middleton

Unleash your creativity
Secrets of creative genius
By Rob Bevan &
Tim Wright

Discover your roots
52 brilliant ideas for exploring your family & local history
By Paul Blake &
Maggie Loughran

For more detailed information on these books and others published by Infinite Ideas please visit www.infideas.com

The best value health book ever

Choose any two titles from below and receive the cheapest one free.

Qty	Title	RRP
	Goddess	£18.99
	Healthy cooking for children	£12.99
	Adventure sports	£12.99
	Skiing and snowboarding	£12.99
	Getting away with it	£6.99
	Re-energise your sex life (2ND EDITION)	£12.99
	Stress proof your life	£12.99
	Upgrade your brain	£12.99
	Inspired creative writing	£12.99
	Unleash your creativity	£12.99
	Detox your finances	£12.99
	Discover your roots	£12.99
	Subtract lowest priced book if ordering two titles	
	Add £2.75 postage per delivery address	
	Final TOTAL	

Name: ....

Delivery address: ....

....

....

....

E-mail:...Tel (in case of problems): ....

By post Fill in all relevant details, cut out or photocopy this page and send along with a cheque made payable to Infinite Ideas. Send to: Best Value Offer, Infinite Ideas, 36 St Giles, Oxford OX1 3LD, UK.

Credit card orders over the telephone Call +44 (0) 1865 514 888. Lines are open 9am to 5pm Monday to Friday. Just mention the promotion code 'BVAD06.'

Please note that no payment will be processed until your order has been dispatched. Goods are dispatched through Royal Mail within 14 working days, when in stock. We never forward personal details on to third parties or bombard you with junk mail. This offer is valid for UK and RoI residents only. Any questions or comments please contact us on 01865 514 888 or email info@infideas.com.